Transformational Coaching for Early Childhood Educators

Transformational
COACHING
for Early Childhood Educators

Constant Hine

Foreword by Ann McClain Terrell

Redleaf Press®
www.redleafpress.org
800-423-8309

Published by Redleaf Press
10 Yorkton Court
St. Paul, MN 55117
www.redleafpress.org

First edition 2019
Senior editor: Heidi Hogg
Managing editor: Douglas Schmitz
Cover design: Louise OFarrell
Cover photograph: Radachynskyi Serhii/Shutterstock.com
Author photograph: Daisy Talleur, Daisy Talleur Photography
Interior design: Paul Nylander | illustrada design
Typeset in Chaparrel Pro 12/16 with Adelle and Shackleton Condensed Titles

Printed in the United States of America
26 25 24 23 22 21 20 19   1 2 3 4 5 6 7 8

Library of Congress Cataloging-in-Publication Data
Names: Hine, Constant, author.
Title: Transformational coaching for early childhood educators / Constant Hine.
Description: St. Paul, MN : Redleaf Press, [2019] | Includes bibliographical references
    and index.
Identifiers: LCCN 2018053165 (print) | LCCN 2018061774 (ebook) |
    ISBN 9781605546414 (ebook) | ISBN 9781605546407 (pbk. : alk. paper)
Subjects: LCSH: Early childhood educators—Training of. | Early childhood teachers—
    Training of. | Mentoring in education.
Classification: LCC LB1775.6 (ebook) | LCC LB1775.6 .H55 2019 (print) |
    DDC 372.21—dc23
LC record available at https://urldefense.proofpoint.com/v2/url?u=https-3A__lccn.loc.
    gov_2018053165&d=DwIFAg&c=euGZstcaTDllvimEN8b7jXrwqOf-v5A_Cdp
    gnVfiiMM&r=gX7U_27BtUCeFTyI7PMJ4yl8ifrCjuxqZQNBnwQelXg&m=IJoFH
    KMRwiEQkvMH4-AwbZSxoH9Rxox0VqZScju1xyg&s=ev-Wvewpp-eGH5c6xN
    _eY9rUSHOkQcGkb4vJ1MoIO18&e=

Printed on acid-free paper

To Sig Hommeyer, my kindergarten teacher, who changed my life forever. I have profound gratitude for Sig's ability to see and polish the gem she saw within me that started my journey.

Contents

Foreword

It is clear from the start of Constant Hine's book, *Transformational Coaching for Early Childhood Educators*, that she is passionate about helping shift the mindsets of early childhood educators from compliant behaviors to inspiring internal personal motivators for learning. This shift creates a system for continuous improvements in educators' own lives and programs.

In my book, *Graceful Leadership in Early Childhood Education*, I shared my professional journey and lessons I learned along the way. Several chapters are dedicated to mentoring from my viewpoint as a mentor and the mentee. I included personal stories of being both because leadership is not a journey we travel alone.

When I hear the words *transformational coaching*, I think of what we hope for when we speak about mentoring, sponsorship or coaching. *Transformation* is the ultimate desired outcome for those that we work with as coaches, and means an outcome of sustainable growth and development for those being coached. However, transformation is a synonym for change, and while change in life is inevitable, it can feel slow and painful at times. Thankfully, in *Transformational Coaching for Early Childhood Educators,* Constant Hine provides us with a road map for navigating that transformation and guides us to an outcome of lasting personal and professional growth.

In my 40-plus year career in early childhood education, I have had the opportunity to experience this kind of coaching from a number of people who I've considered mentors that I now, based on Constant's book, consider "transformational coaches." In those relationships we developed respect, trust, and caring. They provided the guidance and coaching that I benefited from both personally and professionally. Those experiences were indeed transformational and assisted in the upward mobility of my career and provided in some cases, life-changing opportunities. Their influence in my life is one reason I now coach and mentor other early childhood leaders.

In this book, Constant outlines an approach that when implemented allows us to be reflective. To first get to know ourselves at our very core, to examine our values and beliefs, and to understand what motivates our behavior and decision making. As I wrote in my book, "Good leaders are reflective people. The ability to self-reflect, to give serious thought about your own beliefs and behaviors, is an admirable quality and one that all leaders, and those intending to be graceful leaders, should possess."

Constant provides the strategies, accompanied by supporting activities and tools, to help challenge and reawaken early educators' reasons for entering this rewarding field. This form of coaching is ongoing and allows for the desired sustainable change not only for the coach and coachee, but could create true systemic level change.

In our profession of early childhood education, with the challenges of pay equity and turnover, Constant Hine's *Transformational Coaching for Early Childhood Educators* is an excellent resource for supporting the career development of the workforce.

Ann McClain Terrell, award-winning early childhood educator, author of *Graceful Leadership in Early Childhood Education*, and NAEYC governing board president

Acknowledgments

Sig Hommeyer was my kindergarten teacher. She had me for only half a day for one school year, but how she interacted with me changed my life forever. I was only four years old! She loved me unconditionally, and even though I was a young child, she treated me with respect. She saw who I was and helped me see myself as a contribution and as a precious person. I had gotten the message from my family that I was "too loud, too emotional, too dramatic"—basically, too much! I felt that something was wrong with me. I had a lot of energy, and sitting still was not easy for me. I needed a lot of attention for a variety of reasons, and I think I did whatever I needed to try to get that attention. Even though some of my behaviors were somewhat challenging, and I am sure not easy to deal with, Sig Hommeyer always interacted with me as if my energy was a contribution. She didn't recoil at my neediness; she actually leaned in and helped provide the attention I needed. From the day I left her classroom, I never had another teacher who affected me as much as she did. By the age of ten, I knew I wanted to be a teacher. I loved young children, and I wanted to *be* Sig Hommeyer. Thanks to Sig, I did just that—I became an early childhood teacher and then an adult educator.

Sig lit a fire of desire in me that has motivated me and instilled in me the belief that anyone working with young children, or with adults, can change a life forever by how they interact with others, being fully present to each person and respecting their unique way of being human. If you can witness the gem that lies within a person, polish that gem, and help that person see the gem that they are, you are touching a life in the deepest way.

I have been blessed with a professional path in which I work with both young children and adults, allowing me to witness their unfolding as they each become the gem that they are. Sig inspired me then and she still inspires me to this day (I am still in touch with her), not only professionally but also personally and spiritually as I feel the desire and longing to become all of who I can be in the service of others.

I would like to express my gratitude to the many people who have helped me make this book a reality. First, I must thank my patient editor, Cathy

Broberg, who helped and guided me to express myself succinctly yet respectfully maintained my voice. I also am so thankful for her gracious ability and talent to guide the editing process of cutting the mass volume of words into a manageable-sized book. Thank you to the entire team at Redleaf Press for making this a remarkably graceful and considerate experience, especially David Heath, Lindsey Smith, and Heidi Hogg for your guidance and skills, and for answering a million questions.

I have many colleagues, team members, and friends who have accompanied me on this journey of making a book. Thank you, Gretchen Ames, Barbara Blender, Michelle Dupuis, Ann Marie Martin, Anna Florey, Tricia Randall, and Robin Levy. You have been partners and "book doulas" every step of the way: bouncing ideas together with me, giving me feedback on early drafts, transcribing, wading through citation details, helping me stay calm when the deadlines were pressing, and basically encouraging me through the many stages of this creative process. I could not have done it without your help, care, and kindness. I also want to thank the many coachees I have had over the years, for trusting me and for generously sharing yourselves while transforming both professionally and personally, and diligently keeping at it, one step at a time. I have learned so much through working with you, and you have deepened my experience and understanding of what meaningful, "sticky" change requires.

I want to acknowledge my spiritual community of teachers, leaders, and friends, who are my family, with whom I have learned so much and with whom I have done my own deep personal and spiritual work the past twenty-five years. I have been supported to be vulnerable and have learned to have courage to look within and face the changes that need to be made, to have trust and faith that with God all things are possible, and to continue the ongoing journey toward humility and surrender. I have learned meditation practices that provide the daily gift of opening my heart, calming me, and enabling me to think from higher intellience and take action. This is the most foundational, transformational force that guides my life both personally and professionally.

Introduction

This is a book about coaching and making lasting change. It's been percolating throughout my career in early childhood, which began in the classroom, working with two- to five-year-old children, shifted into an adult educator role, and eventually led to coaching. After about ten years of working with educators, I realized that no matter how good the education and professional development were, they were not really changing educators' behaviors. Theory was not manifesting as sustainable changes in professional practices. People often knew what they should be doing, but they were not doing it—for many reasons. This revelation is what prompted me to begin researching what helps people change—really change! And it's also what brought me into the world of coaching. My experience and research verified that as a strategy, coaching was clearly more effective in bringing about change, especially when coupled with education and training. In 2000 there were not many, if any, coaching models to be found in the field, so I learned as much as I could from the corporate community and a few leaders in the K–12 arena. I translated what I could into early education settings, developed my first coaching model for early childhood educators and offered coaching seminars, and in 2004 wrote the book *Coaching for Success*. At the same time, I was also engaging in a personal and spiritual journey to have meaningful breakthroughs in my own life. Through both my personal journey and my desire to make a meaningful contribution professionally to foster sustainable change, I discovered the true power of reflection, inquiry, and vulnerability, and I brought these components into my practices.

Transformational Coaching and Sustainable Change

In the mainstream world of coaching, what is most commonly practiced is a *transactional* approach and methodology of coaching. Transactional coaching occurs when someone who does not like the results they are getting works with a coach to identify new actions that will produce the desired objectives (Terrell and Hughes 2008). The emphasis of transactional coaching is on identifying the goals a person wants to achieve and the actions necessary to accomplish them. In my experience, although this approach can be helpful, it does not support people deeply enough or result in meaningful, lasting change. *Transformational* coaching is an approach that helps people become skillful in the art of self-reflection, to question and examine their foundational perspectives, values, and beliefs that influence their actions or habits. While transformational coaching acknowledges that new actions are indeed needed to generate different outcomes and that setting goals and creating action plans are important, it goes deeper into examining the underlying reasons and motivations behind people's behaviors. Transformational coaching is the approach on which I based the coaching model introduced in this book, the GROOMER Framework for Change™. When I ask coaches what the most challenging barriers are to helping the adult learners they work with—their "coachees"—change, they often cite issues of motivation. The people they support do not seem motivated either to do what they already know how to do or to make changes that are needed. Often these changes are indicated by data gathered from assessment or evaluation tools used to identify "quality" indicators or performance. It is especially challenging to inspire people to change when they are not intrinsically motivated to do so but rather are being asked to change to meet compliance expectations. This is one reason that a transformational approach to coaching is what is really needed to shift the motivational impetus from an external expectation to an internal desire for the change. Cultivating this intrinsic motivation is also what fosters a culture of continuous quality improvement (CQI). Intrinsic motivation can help shift the mind-set of compliance that can accompany and sometimes permeate Quality Rating and Improvement System (QRIS) efforts.

The GROOMER Framework for Change model is a systematic approach to help coaches explore the inner landscape of a person's thinking, behaviors, and actions and to facilitate their learning to improve their practices and achieve meaningful, lasting results. The approach fills the gap between action planning and achieving goals. The components of this model will be described in detail in later chapters. I have always felt privileged to work with early childhood educators because, for the most part, they are a group of people who have a sense of calling, purpose, and even mission. No one enters this field for the pay, that is for sure! So often when I listen to early childhood educators, I hear their passion, desire, and vision. But recently, this has increasingly been masked by stress about the demands of the work. This leads to burnout, conflicts between educators' internal motivations and program expectations or industry standards, and frustration as they try to meet the needs of children and families in a world with increasing individual risk factors and systemic challenges, especially related to issues of equity. It is demanding work, but when it is aligned with an inner desire to contribute and make a difference in the lives of children, coupled with skill sets to meet the demands of the job, it is deeply rewarding. Coaching provides a unique opportunity to help early childhood educators rekindle the reason they came into this field in the first place. It can help them clarify their deepest purpose and desire to make a difference in the lives of children. In addition, when supporting individual early childhood professionals as they commit to creating and practicing habits that foster quality performance, it is quite clear this can only succeed if the programs and systems in which they work are also endeavoring to achieve sustainable results and align professional practices at a systemic level.

Supporting Continuous Quality Improvement

I am passionate about helping both programs and individuals shift from a focus on merely complying with external demands to embracing an internal personal motivation, desire, and passion for learning how to become their best selves and make continuous improvements in their own lives and in the program. There are external industry standards and indicators of best practices that are helpful in guiding professional goals and practices. But unfortunately, the external demands of many programs and quality initiatives, especially publicly funded programs, have become too fixated on meeting compliance outcomes in short time frames, based only on assessment results rather than on the needed and comprehensive efforts to achieve sustainable quality improvement. Igniting passion and purpose in people is essential to fostering a culture of continuous quality improvement (CQI) in our early childhood field. Coaches are in a unique position to develop relationships that can help ignite those passions and support people to thoughtfully walk their journeys. To truly help others, coaches first need to embrace this themselves. They need to personally develop habits of reflection, curiosity, possibility thinking, and willingness to tolerate the discomfort and vulnerability of change. They need to find the courage to challenge and want more for themselves, the educators they support, the children and families they serve, the programs where they work, and the systems that invest in the delivery of services to young children.

The Power of Reflection

The power of reflection is the foundational philosophy of this book and the GROOMER Framework for Change model. Through their own reflection, coaches can deepen facilitation and coaching skills that help other people learn how to expand their own awareness. It is equally important to facilitate a learner's ability to make conscious and intentional decisions to solve their own problems, to learn how to make changes to grow, and to learn and develop personally and professionally. Reflection is the heart of conscious transformational coaching to groom change skills and facilitate the change process.

Intentional Decision-Making

The first step to being effective as a coach, then, is to do your own work, become self-aware, and walk your talk. It's critical to build strong habits of reflective practice about your own life and your own professional practices, and you will need to examine and recognize whether you are indeed being effective at facilitating learning and change in others. The second step is to apply your awareness to make intentional choices about which strategies and tools you use to facilitate others through their own change process. The third step is to examine whether the strategies you are using actually have the impact you intend.

MY PERSONAL JOURNEY LEARNING TO CHANGE

Several years ago, I suffered a severe concussion after slipping on a wet sidewalk. This resulted in a mild brain injury that took well over two years to recover from. I learned a lot about change during my recovery from that accident. As my brain healed, my energy level was greatly reduced, so I had to slow down and change many of my basic daily habits. This required a lot of awareness of what I was doing, how long a task took, how much energy it required, and how much stimuli I could tolerate. As difficult as all this was, in some ways the accident was the unexpected answer to my prayers. Throughout the year before my injury, I had talked about needing to create a more balanced lifestyle with fewer work hours and more time for self-care, family and friends, and my spiritual practices. I had the desire for this but not enough commitment to actually take action. With the concussion, I was forced to slow down. Another thing I learned from this time is that small, seemingly insignificant actions and thoughts repeated daily really do result in big changes that stick over time. I also came to see that there is a pattern and flow to how we change, and that pattern includes ebbs and flows, plateaus, and even setbacks. Although my experience resulted from a medical situation, the change process is similar whether it is about physical recovery or emotional, spiritual, personal, or professional situations. The habits I developed during my recovery created a new, much healthier lifestyle for me. My recovery required reflection, reframing attitudes, and being consistent in small daily actions. It also taught me never to give up! Sometimes we know we want to change some professional practices, but the idea of going through with the effort is daunting. Sometimes the final push for taking action may come from an external demand, such as new standards or program goals we need to comply with. When this happens, your attitude and perception about the change will be crucial to your success. The experience of recovering from my concussion affected my thoughts, approaches, and professional practices about coaching. It refined my understanding of how best to facilitate change, especially change that is challenging and requires a lot of practice to really stick. For the previous fifteen years, I had been using my original coaching model, the Framework for Thinking. Through my recovery experience, I saw the need to add a few more components to the process of helping people reflect and achieve lasting change. I made those additions and created the seven-component GROOMER Framework for Change model.

Intention for This Book

I have found that coaching is one of the most significant strategies for cultivating transformational change in both individuals and organizations. My intention and objective with this book is to offer a coaching model with practical facilitation strategies and tools that foster conscious quality improvements and meaningful change that "sticks" over time for both individuals and, systemically, for programs. Each chapter of this book includes the following:

- activities, tools, and skills for practicing the strategies discussed

- reflective practices to expand your awareness, perceptions, and skill mastery of your own coaching practices

- a Reflection in Action section, which will summarize the chapter's key messages and ask sequential questions about what you learned and how that affected your thinking, professional practices, and any actions you might want to take

These sequential questions are the core of the Technology of Participation (ToP) methodology that takes reflection deeper into the topic. As authors Wayne and Jo Nelson (2017) explain in their book *Getting to the Bottom of ToP*, "Each level is a distinct mode of thinking dominated by a particular type of *information* processing." This reflection method is not only for your own learning but also for use in facilitating reflective conversation with coachees.

- The Objective step is the *what* (basic data).

- The Reflective step is the *gut* (associations, connections, relationships, and feelings related to the topic).

- The Interpretive step is the *so what* (significance, meaning, importance, and implications).

- The Decisional step is the *now what* (conclusions and decisions).

Throughout this book, you'll see many example forms, worksheets, and activities. Blank copies are available to download at www.redleafpress.org /transformationalcoaching. You can use these forms as often as you like in your coaching work.

This book is designed as an interactive tool to help you learn to connect theory to practice by engaging with the content in a way that is meaningful for you. Whether you are new to coaching or have years of experience, I hope you will join me in this journey of continuous exploration, investigation, and improvement in expanding our knowledge, skills, experience, and professional practices about how to facilitate sustainable change in ourselves and others. We all deserve to take the time to reflect, think, and learn what real, lasting change requires. The children deserve this commitment from us, and the world needs conscious people to contribute their gifts and care to others.

The Role of the Coach

Creating a new lifestyle or professional practice is like growing a garden. You have to plant, cultivate, and harvest. Cultivating can only happen over the course of time. Lasting, "sticky" change comes from the effort devoted to the cultivation process. The GROOMER Framework for Change model introduced in this book includes all the necessary components to facilitate the whole journey of the change cycle—from planning to planting to cultivation and, finally, to harvest. As with gardening, you can't pull that new fledgling plant up any faster than its own growth process. Adding external pressure doesn't help. What does help is cultivating through reflection, watering the soil with encouragement, and weeding out limiting or negative thinking that is toxic to growth. The coach's role is to be a partner, or cogardener, with the people they support—their coachees. A coach's intention is to groom people's ability to change and learn with skill and, hopefully, some grace.

The process of trial and error that occurs as new ideas or practices are implemented produces a great deal of learning opportunities through the cultivation that happens over time, and takes time. Change is not just about setting a goal or creating a plan. Making real change also requires tolerating the discomfort of not necessarily getting it right or getting quick results. Information alone does not change behavior; this requires reflection and practice over time. One of the skills required to cultivate change is the ability to tolerate the discomfort of practicing small, daily habits, not unlike pulling weeds. It's not always glamorous. This is true for your own transformation and the deepening of your professional practices, and it's true for those you support. A coach's role as a change agent is to help people tolerate discomfort and vulnerability while they are dealing with change, practicing new habits, experiencing failures, trying things out for the first time when not knowing what the results are going to be, and taking what might seem like insignificant small steps. But these small steps are what create sustainable changes and foster the adoption of best practices as consistent habits for early childhood educators.

> *"Simple daily disciplines—little productive actions, repeated consistently over time—add up to the difference between failure and success."*
> —*Jeff Olson,* The Slight Edge

This is where the rubber really hits the road. While testing new ideas, implementing solutions, and experimenting with possible options, coaches support their coachees to observe, gather data, and document their results and progress. Then coaches help them use this information to reflect and evaluate to make data-driven decisions for how to finalize solutions, create lasting habits, and/or proceed to the next level of quality improvement. Following are some coaching habits to cultivate sustainable change:

- Cultivate trusting relationships that promote mutual respect and create a safe container for learning.

- Practice and model clear and complete communication.

- Adopt the neutral position of observer of yourself, your thoughts, your emotions, and your actions to increase your own awareness. Facilitate coachees to neutrally observe themselves to gather data and information, and to document what they think, how they feel and behave, and what their habits of practice are. Encourage educators to evaluate whether their actions and habits are effective or not, and how to make informed decisions about how to improve and make positive changes. Determine whether there is an alignment between the requirements and expectations of the coach and the coaching initiative with the needs and expectations of the coachee.

Build Trust and Partnership

Relationships are the foundation for all learning. Coaches must build trusting and respectful partnerships with the people they coach. Having a humble attitude and remembering that you are asking to be a partner who enters into the person's inner world is important. Accompanying someone in their learning journey is a privilege, which can be both a vulnerable and joyful experience. Here are some guidelines for building trust and partnership:

- Create a safe place to reflect. Build trust through transparent communication, without judgment or unspoken expectations.

- Be curious and explore how the coachee views the world. What is their story or philosophy, especially as it relates to education and their professional identity as an educator and as a learner?

- Inquire about what the coachee's interests and hopes are for the children they serve. Gain an understanding of their perceptions, values, and beliefs.

- Clarify how they learn best, and build on their personal strengths and identify weaknesses to better individualize.

- Identify the coachee's risk tolerance, and explore how to help them tolerate the discomfort of change.

- Discern what stage of change they are in about their current problem, goal, or situation.

- Demonstrate an appreciation for the coachee's perspective, even when it is different from your own.

- Create a safe container for a collaborative inquiry, examination, and discussion about the issues related to equity, culture, power, privilege, and bias, which are influential in establishing rapport and relationship between the coach and coachee. Examine how these equity issues influence your own and the coachee's professional practices, and how they affect the workplace and community as related to working with supervisors, colleagues, children, and families.

- Transfer the power to the coachee as often as possible.

- Practice the art of "followership" by inquiring with respect and following the coachee's lead, even if there are specific expectations for focus areas.

- Provide ongoing support for new behaviors and actions, focusing on learning opportunities and progress even when outcomes are disappointing.

- Provide avenues for the coachee to give feedback and evaluate the coach, the coaching relationship, and the effectiveness of the coaching experience.

Set the Foundation and Establish Clear Agreements

To foster a strong partnership, the coach will want to develop a context for understanding the purpose of coaching, the coaching relationship, and clarify the roles and responsibilities of both the coach and the coachee. Create a framework that aligns the requirements and expectations of the coach and the coaching initiative with the needs and expectations of the coachee, which includes mutually setting goals and coaching agendas to meet all stakeholder needs. Some of this will happen at the beginning of a coaching relationship when establishing an understanding and foundation for the partnership. Some agreements will continue to develop, unfold, and adapt in response to changing needs throughout the coaching relationship. The following points can help set the foundation and establish clear coaching agreement:

- Discuss mutual expectations of and for the coach and coachee, any requirements of the coaching relationship, including the framework and goals of the coaching initiative and the roles of any other parties (such as funders, project coordinators, or evaluators).

- Create a mutually understood policy for
  - o   time commitments (duration of relationship, frequency and length of appointments),
  - o   scheduling when and how to meet (onsite or remote), cancelation notification and timeframes,
  - o   coachee availability support (arranging for classroom coverage when necessary, and meeting setting),
  - o   preferred mode of communication and how to best reach each other,
  - o   giving and receiving feedback,
  - o   follow-through on tasks,
  - o   confidentiality (who is included in the meeting, receives session notes, assessment results, etc.),
  - o   and ethical responsibilities and dilemmas.

- Discuss criteria for measures of success, reporting requirements, and processes or forms that will help document progress, success, and outcomes.

- If the coachee is participating in more than one coaching initiative or has multiple coaches, help clarify and establish clear lines of communication between coaching efforts.

- Discuss the philosophical foundation of the coaching partnership and share the coaching model or approach to be used.

Be a Model and Walk the Talk!

To be effective, coaches need to examine and improve their own personal habits and professional practices so they are able to authentically model reflective and professional practices for their coachees. This parallel process is important because coaches want to behave and interact with coachees in the same manner that they hope their coachees will interact with children, families, and colleagues.

- Model how you deal with change, and share your own process to make change less intimidating.

- Be willing to embrace the change process, make and share mistakes, and innovate yourself.

- Be willing and able to ask tough questions, challenge the coachee's thinking, and expand the coachee's reflections about roadblocks— and bust any barriers in the process.

- Be prepared for things to move slowly. Thinking takes time and change is a process that happens over time.

Normalize the Challenges of the Change Process

The coach is like a guide for the coachee, helping navigate the process of change. One of the coach's more critical roles is to explain and normalize the change process. You will need to explain and prepare people and programs for what they might encounter, to help them recognize that they are in an ongoing process, and to empower them to engage in the process with curiosity rather than fear.

The following points about the change process are important to share and discuss with individuals and programs:

- Change is a process, not a destination or an event. Change takes time and is a long-term endeavor that may at times require patience.

- It's important to allow enough time to make changes that are sustainable.

- It's normal for coachees to feel vulnerable or unsure of themselves at times while making changes, and they will need to tolerate discomfort. Discomfort does not mean that something is wrong.

- Be willing to shift the coachees' perspectives of challenges and mistakes, and see them as a normal part of the change process.

- It's okay not to know everything; keep an open mind. Coachees may have to reevaluate long-held beliefs, assumptions, and expectations.

- Coachees will examine their readiness for change and how to stretch their risk tolerance. To learn is to change, and change happens by practicing the process of changing.

Reframe CQI as a Process

The movement in the field to focus on CQI helps direct our attention and goals toward developing program cultures that embrace change as a process, not just an event but something that happens over time. Quality is actually an ongoing process that never ends, and it demands professional rigor of reflection, inquiry, questioning, investigation, collaboration, evaluation, experimentation, and refinement to develop the best ways to meet the diverse needs of children and families with an equitable approach. Coaching empowers professionals to do just that. Coaching is critical to help early childhood professionals (from funders, directors, classroom teachers, providers, and paraprofessionals) internalize and own what quality means in terms of daily practices and interactions, and to break free from a fear-based culture of compliance.

The movement toward improving quality in early childhood programs has been a noble and worthy cause, but it's important to avoid overstressing only the measurement of quality when what's really important is to develop a systematic approach to investing in the strategies and habits of quality improvement. Local or state quality initiatives often rely on several assessments to rate programs as part of a QRIS. Typically programs need to achieve a certain score to get a good quality rating and sometimes to obtain specific funding options. The pressure to comply with these requirements and attain high scores has contributed to the impression that quality is merely a product, based solely on something that can be attained by a quantitative assessment rating alone. Coaches often feel pressured to coach or teach to the test when they are asked by teachers, directors, funders, and providers to help them get a good score on an assessment. Coaching can then become an event-based experience rather than an ongoing journey to become "better at getting better" at what we do. This is a dilemma for coaches who must determine how to help programs achieve high ratings while also helping educators do the deep work of understanding and implementing daily professional practices that actually improve the quality of children's and families' experiences. Implementing change management using facilitation skills is certainly part of the coach's role as an agent of change.

"One major purpose of a QRIS is to recognize quality and promote a culture of continuous improvement among providers. The rating is not a destination; it is a set of benchmarks along a pathway of ongoing improvement."
—Anne Mitchell, Alliance for Early Childhood Finance

Pause & Reflect

How can you strengthen or shift your perspective to embrace change as a process instead of being overly focused on outcomes?

_____

_____

_____

_____

_____

Billie Young (2017, 3), in the report *Continuous Quality Improvement in Early Childhood and School Age Programs*, gives a comprehensive definition of CQI:

> Continuous Quality Improvement (CQI) is a process which ensures that organizations and their partners are systemic and intentional about improving services and practices and increasing positive outcomes for children and families. CQI is optimally seated in an organizational culture that has a common vision, shared values and beliefs, and a commitment to ongoing quality improvement. CQI is reflective, cyclical and data-driven; it is proactive, not reactive. It goes beyond merely meeting externally applied standards and moves the lever for change internally. Participants control the process themselves through continuous learning and a dedication to "getting better at getting better."

The CQI approach supports efforts to intentionally include the perspectives, needs, and voices of all stakeholders in the decision-making and implementation process to improve quality. Coaches can play an important leadership role in helping the industry flip the switch from exclusionary—voices of privileged authority operating in disconnected silos—to broadcasting and shedding light on the diverse voices of educators working at the ground level who need to be heard, respected, and empowered with equity. Coaches often find themselves right in the middle of the funders and agencies and the educators in the field. They may end up having to communicate and translate external demands to providers. At the same time, coaches often are in a key position to enlighten funders and agencies about the current needs and conditions in the field and be the voice representing the provider, teacher, and program. Bridging this divide is important to the ongoing efforts to support quality improvement so children, families, and educators can thrive. Here are some key points for coaches to understand, embrace, and communicate regarding a CQI approach. CQI can be defined as

- not a destination but a journey;

- an ongoing cyclical process between reflection, experimentation, documentation, and refinement;

- a process of including reflection as part of regular professional practices at all levels of a program or organization;

Chapter 1

Hot Tip

The National Center on Quality Teaching and Learning identified the following indicators of a culture of CQI (2011):

- curiosity
- reflection
- tolerance of failure and vulnerability
- use of feedback
- systems thinking

- a shift from focusing on only the end product to including process and milestones of progress;

- an ongoing process that happens over time;

- a shift from externally driven (compliance) to internally motivated desire and commitment;

- balance between individual effort and team effort;

- including all stakeholder voices and perspectives in the decision-making process (board, management, employees, families, children, and other partners);

- decision-making based on collected data and documentation of quality, including both quantitative and qualitative data;

- providing the best possible services and outcomes for the people being served—the children and families; and

- to get better and better at getting better and better.

Use the seven components of the GROOMER Framework for Change Model (see chapter 3) as a guideline to facilitate the ongoing change process to foster CQI at the individual and systems levels:

G—GOAL: Clarifying visions and goals and specifying criteria for success

R—REALITY: Identifying the reality of current practices—what works and what doesn't

O—OPTION: Identifying options and possibilities for how to close the gap between current practices and desired results

O—OBSTACLE: Identifying any obstacles and barriers

M—MOBILIZE: Mobilizing and developing action plans

E—EXPERIMENT: Experimenting by implementing plans and testing options and ideas

R—REFINE: Refining solutions and modifying plans, to clarify the next steps or levels necessary to improve quality and professional practices

⯑ ⯑

COMPARE AND CONTRAST QRIS AND CQI

Reflect on your own experiences and knowledge and, in your own words, describe the focus of QRIS and how that differs from the focus of a CQI approach. Identify where they overlap and what they have in common. Use this activity as an opportunity to clarify how you might discuss this with a coachee or a program you coach.

QRIS

_____

_____

_____

_____

CQI

_____

_____

_____

_____

Both

_____

_____

_____

_____

⯑ ⯑

Assess the Coachee's Readiness for Change

Coaches are like doulas or midwives who accompany people through the change process. Coachees have varying degrees of willingness and readiness for change. It is typical for a coachee to have unbalanced, variable, or even contradictory levels of readiness for change depending on the focus area or topic. One person can be very proactive and motivated to make changes in several areas of life, but in one specific area, they may be more hesitant, afraid, or not yet ready. It is important for coaches to clarify each coachee's willingness and readiness for change in each area that might need change, a goal, or an action plan. Clinical psychologists and researchers James Prochaska, John Norcross, and Carlo DiClemente (1994) studied how people intentionally change and discovered there is a structure to change. They were able to identify that successful self-changing follows a predictable course. In their book *Changing for Good*, they introduce the six distinct, well-defined stages of change:

1. Precontemplation—resisting change
2. Contemplation—change on the horizon
3. Preparation—getting ready
4. Action—time to move
5. Maintenance—staying there
6. Relapse—lapse or setback

The Six Stages of Change model is helpful to identify how to work with people given their risk tolerance and readiness for change. These stages are applicable to any topic, regardless of the problem or specific issue. The authors also learned that to successfully move through each of these stages toward a resolution or lasting change, it is important to use different and unique kinds of interventions or facilitation approaches at each stage.

□ □

THE SIX STAGES OF CHANGE READINESS ASSESSMENT

Circle yes or no after each sentence, then use the next section to help assess the stage either you or someone else is in for changing a particular problem behavior.

1. I solved my problem more than six months ago.   Y   N

2. I have taken action on my problem within the past six months.   Y   N

3. I am intending to take action in the next month.   Y   N

4. I am intending to take action in the next six months.   Y   N

If you answered no to all statements, you are at the precontemplation stage.

If you answered yes to statement 4 and no to all others, you are at contemplation.

If you answered yes to statements 3 and 4 and no to the others, you are at preparation.

If you answered yes to statement 2 and no to statement 1, you are at action.

If you truthfully answered yes to statement 1, you are at maintenance.

□ □

This model can be very useful in identifying what stage of change a person is in. Having this knowledge helps coaches effectively use targeted tools to guide coachees through the change process using the GROOMER Framework for Change. This can be particularly important when working with people who say they will make changes but do not actually follow through. Assessing their readiness for change and reconsidering whether the facilitation strategies you have been using are helping or are actually contributing to their resistance is important. Resistance to change indicates a motivational obstacle. The role of a coach, like a gardener, is multifaceted in order to cultivate change. It requires a commitment to one's own continuous improvement to learn effective facilitation strategies. In addition, it requires gaining the knowledge, understanding, skills, and motivation to patiently and intentionally support others to do the same.

Reflection in Action

Take time to reflect on what you learned in this chapter and its impact on and value for you.

_____

_____

_____

Key messages:

- Build trust and partnership.
- Set the foundation and establish clear agreements.
- Model and walk the walk.
- Normalize the change process.
- Reframe continuous quality improvement (CQI) as a process.
- Assess the coachee's readiness for change by using the Six Stages of Change to intentionally facilitate change.

Objective: What are key words or phrases, quotes, concepts, stories, activities, or ideas that stand out or stick for you personally?

_____

_____

Reflective: What part of this feels affirming or inspiring? What aspect feels like a stretch or might be challenging for you?

_____

_____

Interpretive: What was most relevant and meaningful for you? How does this information affect your work or coaching practices?

_____

_____

Decisional: What implications does this have for your actions in the future? What are you most committed to putting into action?

_____

_____

Habits of Reflection

Reflection is the heart of change and the process of cultivating more-effective personal habits and professional practices. Becoming aware through reflection is the first step to change. It makes sense, then, that a major aspect of coaching is to cultivate self-reflection in coachees and to link the resulting awareness with making intentional choices to achieve goals. The more you can cultivate habits of reflection, the more people will build positive professional daily habits to support their quality improvement and mastery of their professional practices.

Helping people cultivate habits of reflection is how coaches can most effectively invest their time to facilitate sustainable change. This is a much more proactive approach than having to repeatedly give advice or implement intervention strategies once there is resistance, an obstacle, or a barrier to the change process. The more coachees reflect, the less likely they are to encounter habitual obstacles and barriers that require repeated intervention. While any change process includes challenges, by cultivating habits of reflection an individual can reduce the intensity and frequency of challenges, especially related to lack of awareness, negative thinking, and lack of motivation. As change agent partners, coaches help people on this discovery journey cultivate and tend to their garden of learning and grow intentional professional practices.

Helping people become more reflective is essentially the purpose of coaching—to help others become more aware, solve their own problems, expand the potential of their own performance, and help them learn, rather than advising them or telling them what to do.

Coaches facilitate and help coachees

- deepen and broaden their thinking and expand perceptions;

- foster creative critical thinking skills;

- clarify their motivation and willingness to change;

- foster metacognitive thinking—to think about thinking and the link between their thoughts, emotions, the choices they make, and the results;

19

- explore and validate the reliability of their beliefs;

- reassess the impact of their beliefs and values;

- develop more consistent and empowering beliefs;

- identify filters, assumptions, fears, judgments, or inferences that create obstacles or hinder their ability to find positive solutions or adopt positive habits;

- make informed decisions based on data and documentation; and

- increase their ability to consciously choose and change their own performance to achieve their desired outcomes.

$$\text{\emph{Reflection}} \quad + \quad \text{\emph{Revisions of a Frame of Reference}} \quad = \quad \text{\emph{Paradigm Shifts (Sustainable Change)}}$$

The Power of Reflection

Intentional transformational coaching is subtler and more complex than just helping people set goals and make action plans. Our life journeys and experiences, not just our professional experiences, contribute to our philosophy and influence how we approach anything we do. To make a change, whether due to social or professional demands, we need to become more conscious of and effective in the way we approach what we do. Thinking takes time! Coaches need to allow time and respect purposeful pauses for people to reflect.

"Given the emotionally evocative nature and the complexity of work with very young children and families who are vulnerable, it is imperative that practitioners across disciplines have time to pause and reflect."
—Deborah Weatherston, Robert F. Weigand, and Barbara Weigand, "Reflective Supervision," Zero to Three

It is part of the human experience to make meaning of our experiences. We make meaning through the way we string together and interpret our personal and cultural perceptions, experiences, values, and feelings. People are meaning-making machines, and we create meaning structures through critical reflection of our experiences, by engaging in dialogue with others, and by purposefully reassessing the impact and foundation of our beliefs and values. A frame of reference is made up of assumptions and expectations that frame a person's or group's unspoken point of view and influence their thinking, beliefs, and actions. It is as if each person has a picture frame through which they view the world and themselves; this is the individual's frame of reference. The shape and size of each frame is created by the person's assumptions, expectations, experiences, thoughts, beliefs, and actions, all of which continue to influence what one experiences. This frame of reference is how we make meaning. A person's frame of reference is their unique point of view through which they relate new experiences to their past learning. Knowing your frame of reference is important; otherwise you might make choices unconsciously with little awareness. This can result in regrettable actions, create ineffective practices, and cause separation in your relationships.

The change process occurs within a person's individual or a group's collective frame of reference. By revising your frame of reference, combined with reflecting on new experiences, a transformation in your perspective—a paradigm shift—can take place. In 1978 Jack Mezirow introduced the theory of transformative learning that explained how adults change the way they interpret their world. This theory is considered uniquely adult—that is, grounded in human communication, where "learning is understood as the process of using a prior interpretation to construe a new or revised interpretation of meaning of one's experience in order to guide future action" (Mezirow 1996). Essentially, creating a paradigm shift cultivates sustainable learning and sticky change. Gaining self-awareness requires examining the essential elements of our frame of reference in order to understand what is creating our beliefs and values, and how this motivates our professional practices.

Practice Reflection for Response-able Coaching

In the book *The Thinking Teacher*, Sandra Heidemann, Beth Menninga, and Claire Chang (2016, 71) write about how important it is for early educators to respect themselves as professionals: "Think of your professional identity as a story you are creating," they urge. "That story forms a picture of how you see yourself as a teacher, how effective you feel, how you define your style of teaching, and what you see as your strengths and weaknesses in the classroom. It is also the story of how you take what you know about learning and teaching and bring it to life in your own way." To navigate the journey of change both personally and professionally, both coaches and coachees must take time to reflect on their personal life experiences, professional experiences, and foundational values, and how they have been affected by these experiences. This reflection contributes to a deeper understanding of an individual's professional identity or philosophy. Coaches need to consider how their values and thoughts are affecting their current professional experiences and practices as coaches. Doing your own reflective work is essential before you can authentically help others do theirs. Coaching supports the process required to establish meaningful professional goals, consider possible solutions, and become willing to take risks to change. When coaches perceive themselves as whole beings and reflect on how they bring who they are to what they do, it can have a profound impact on their ability to truly serve the educators, children, families, and staff they work with. This requires courage and practice. Reflecting on their own frame of reference helps coaches be both respectful of and responsive to the people they support. To be self-responsible and accountable for their own actions, coaches should do the following:

- Become aware of their own "operating systems" that infuse their meaning-making mechanisms, perceptions, and eventual actions.

- Examine if their values, beliefs, and behaviors are aligned with and consistent with their personal intentions and professional objectives.

- Explore and validate the reliability of their values and beliefs, and the impact they have on their behaviors, actions, and ability to make informed decisions.

Our meaning structure also influences how we interpret interactions with others and what we assign importance to. It affects our ability to be empathetic toward others, especially those who may have differing values, cultural issues, or challenges in life. Being aware of one's frame of reference clearly affects a coach's ability to be effective.

My Paradigm Shift

Early in my career, my unexamined beliefs, strengths, and biases (my frame of reference) affected my professional practices and my ability to be an effective mentor teacher. From this experience, I had an important awakening that shifted my paradigm and caused me to revise my frame of reference. Ultimately this changed the course of my personal journey and professional career.

FROM INSTINCTIVE TO CONSCIOUS DECISION-MAKING

As a new preschool teacher with only a couple years of experience, I was asked to be a mentor teacher. My director asked me to do this because she said I was a naturally good teacher. In particular I was good at dealing with the challenging behaviors of children. But I didn't really know what I did that made me successful. My approach was more of an instinctive or gut response—not from conscious awareness. When I became a mentor teacher, I had to learn how to articulate what I did to teach another person how to do that same thing. This required reflection on my part and, ultimately, a shift in my frame of reference. For example, I told my student teacher to watch a particular child because I could tell he was about to act out. She asked me in a bewildered voice, "How did you know he was about to act out?" I looked at her oddly, wondering why she didn't see it. But in that moment, I realized she actually didn't see what I was seeing. This experience forced me to reflect on how I knew what I knew and what I did. With reflection, I realized I could read body language—when this child got red in the face and tightened his body, it meant he was upset. Reflecting and thinking about this helped me gain a new perspective, and I looked at my practices from a more critical and intentional place. This helped me witness some of my previously unseen inherent strengths, assumptions about how children learn, and beliefs I had about "challenging" behaviors. I realized some of my beliefs and assumptions were a little nonconformist. Since I was myself labeled a challenging child, I realized I had an extra level of empathy for children with challenging behaviors; I wasn't triggered by them. I was curious about what unmet needs were causing the behavior and investigated how I could help. I remembered choosing to act out as a child (for example, talking to a child nearby or even pinching someone) rather than being shamed in class for not understanding the content being studied. I knew those challenging behaviors would prompt the teacher to send me to the principal's office. My challenging behavior was the *solution* to my problem of feeling embarrassed about not understanding the lesson and thinking I was stupid. I preferred getting in trouble to feeling shame about not knowing the subject matter. But until I began to think reflectively and critically about my teaching practices, I didn't realize how my personal experiences had influenced my understanding that children act out as a way to solve a problem, subsequently influencing my approach to positive guidance and discipline. This reflective practice also helped me recognize that I had the individual strength of interpersonal intelligence, which helped me read body language in order to anticipate children's actions. Until I stopped to reflect, those strengths, beliefs, and assumptions were all unknowingly part of my frame of reference, and I was blindly operating from them.

Once I gained this expanded view of myself—of my beliefs about teaching and learning—and engaged in a dialogue with the student teacher, I became both a better teacher and mentor. I was able to practice better ways of teaching and articulating what I was doing and why to support my student teacher. This experience changed not only my own teaching practices by making me more intentional and conscientious, but also how I worked with student teachers in the future.

Explore Frames of Reference to Expand Awareness

This experience changed me more fundamentally in another way as well. I learned the power of critical reflection and metacognition (to think about my thinking), and the impact that my thoughts, beliefs, and assumptions had on my professional practices. I also learned that to do that kind of critical, reflective thinking, I needed to talk with others about what I was discovering. This dialogue helped me gain a better perspective of my own thinking. It was different from just having a thought inside my head, which didn't give me enough distance or perspective. These conversations were a rich garden from which I could grow and harvest a new attitude of inquiry, of asking new questions. The process expanded my passion for teaching and my sense of possibilities about learning, and it reframed my worldview. This gave me a new perspective for how to continue the change and learning process in itself, beyond helping student teachers learn how to deal with children's challenging behaviors. I learned how to learn with conscious intentionality, and that seemed to open a whole new world. It was a paradigm change—not to just be a passenger learner, but to see that I had the power to drive and choose the direction of my learning. It also influenced my choice to leave the classroom and increased my desire and motivation to work with adult educators. This continues to affect my current work as a coach as I ponder how to facilitate this kind of reflection and introspection in other coaches and educators most effectively .

"Unlike puppets, we have the possibility of stopping in our movements, looking up and perceiving the machinery by which we have been moved. In this act lies the first step towards freedom."
—*Peter Berger,* Invitation to Sociology: A Humanistic Perspective

Modeling and facilitating this reflective critical thinking and inquiry is the heart of transformational coaching that will result in lasting change. Helping educators see how their frame of reference influences their choices and practices can open windows to new horizons. From those new vistas, they can make conscious decisions to positively influence and create the quality of the education and care they want to provide children and families. Coaches have the privilege of being able to witness and facilitate transformational learning in others as they experiment with how

How do I know if what I am doing is working?

_____

_____

_____

_____

_____

Pause & Reflect

to fulfill their sense of purpose and reach their visions and goals personally and professionally.

The following My Frame of Reference activity is designed to help you identify the lens through which you perceive, interpret, and create meaning. It is also important to determine if you have "inherited" some values that may not fully align with or support who you aspire to be or your current professional practices. You may have learned values from your family that are actually barriers to being successful professionally. But through reflection, you can make conscious choices about your values, beliefs, and thoughts. You do not have to be a victim of your own frame of reference. You have a choice about what you believe, how you think, and how you act.

I have provided my personal frame of reference to give you an example of the kinds of things you might want to include in your own reflection, discovery, and writing. You'll want to summarize the key influencers that affect you. Or you might identify any "rules to live by" that you have, which sometimes are favorite sayings, such as "If you don't have anything nice to say, don't say anything at all." That idiom captures an important value. Contemplating whether the values you identify still serve you and if you still intentionally choose to allow them to influence you is important. Some you will likely feel strongly aligned with, and some may cause you to pause and reconsider.

Becoming self-aware takes courage and practice, but the benefits and values can affect coaches way beyond their professional lives. When coaches practice this parallel process of reflecting and neutrally observing their own and their coachee's thoughts and actions to make informed decisions, it allows coaches to model for educators the very habits they are encouraging them to develop. Practicing facilitation and coaching skills to help people reflect is the foundational philosophy of this book and the GROOMER Framework for Change Model. Remember, a coach's role is to

Beliefs Assumptions Values

Race **Nationality** **Education & Learning Experiences**

Past Experiences **Socioeconomic** **Gender**

Constant's Frame of Reference

I am a white divorced woman who was raised in an upper-middle-income family in a predominantly white midwestern community in the 1960s counterculture. I have divorced parents, five birth siblings, and four stepsiblings. My parents' alternative, liberal values and lifestyle influenced my political, social, and personal values.

I had the *best* kindergarten teacher who changed my life and made me want to be a teacher. Despite this strong start, my educational journey was not easy. I had difficulty learning in school and was in pullout reading and speech therapy in grade school. I hated school and thought I was dumb. I attended a combination of public schools, an alternative school, and private schools. I traveled for two years between high school and college.

In college I discovered a love of learning—and that I was actually smart—and got a master's degree. My primary ways of being smart are visual, interpersonal, and verbal intelligences. Because of my experience, I believe children are competent and to be trusted. I have been part of a spiritual meditation community for over twenty-five years, and I meditate daily. My spiritual life influences my decision-making and includes practicing self-reflection and facing illusory aspects of my character to make intentional changes to become my best self. I have both a spiritual coach and a business coach who help me self-reflect, set goals, create action plans, and make changes in my personal, spiritual, and professional daily habits. I value self-examination and "doing my work" to practice and be aligned with what I value.

There have been thirteen deaths in my immediate family, and I have been at the bedside for six deaths. This has greatly affected my perceptions of life and my acceptance of pain and grief as part of life's fabric. I was deeply affected by the death of my sister, who was my best friend.

I tend to be an optimist and have a positive attitude. I practice writing "daily gratitudes."

I have a lot of energy and need to work at being self-responsible for my health, well-being, and lifestyle pacing.

I value friendship and have friends all over the world.

I believe in the power of love to transform individuals and the world.

Culture Family Religion

Beliefs   **Assumptions**   **Values**

My Frame of Reference

Instructions: Write anything that is part of your own frame of reference—what influences how you view the world. Write your filters, values, past experiences, culture, gender, ethnicity, and so on in the frame below. Be concrete and specific. Do not worry about writing in complete sentences.

Race   **Nationality**   **Education & Learning Experiences**

Past Experiences   **Socioeconomic**   **Gender**

Culture   **Family**   **Religion**

empower people to learn the actual process of learning *how* to reflect, *how* to make conscious and intentional decisions to solve their own problems, and to be responsible for their own learning by learning *how* to change. The purpose of transformational coaching is to facilitate meaningful change.

In his book *The Slight Edge*, Jeff Olson states that the key ingredient to success and lasting change is a person's philosophy—this is what provides the "slight edge." He writes:

> The actions, the what-to-do and how-to-do its, is not enough, because it is the attitude behind the actions that keep those actions in place. . . . To find the path to success, you have to back up one more step. It is the understanding behind the attitudes that are behind the actions. It is the philosophy. That's the missing ingredient, the secret ingredient. The first ingredient. Your philosophy is what you know, how you hold what you know, and how it affects what you do. . . . The slight edge is the first ingredient, the catalyst you need that makes all the how-tos work. . . . Your philosophy creates your attitudes, your actions, your results—create your life. (Olson 2013, 20)

Pause & Reflect

What is your professional philosophy? Or what is your philosophy of coaching?

_____

_____

_____

_____

_____

_____

Perception Is Power

Once again, how we perceive our experiences, ourselves, other people, and basically everything in the world around us comes from our filters—our frame of reference. When we take responsibility for our perceptions, we are able to make radical changes—we are empowered to make life choices that affect everything! The key to being self-empowered, rather than a victim of circumstances, is being responsible for your perceptions. Most everything

Perceptions Creating Results

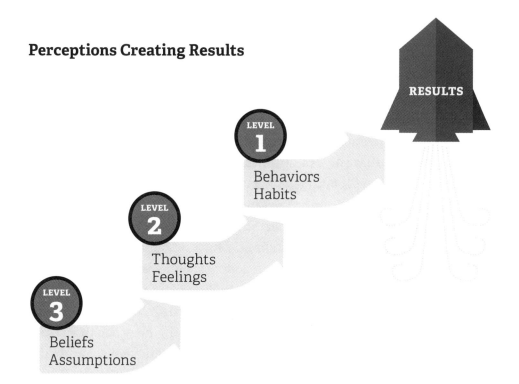

in this world is not in your control. However, every single bit of how you choose to perceive a situation is totally within your control. Nobody forces you to perceive anything. What you decide to perceive is your choice. Choose intentionally and consciously!

Your beliefs and values create your thoughts. Your thoughts elicit your feelings—they don't just happen to you. Feelings come from what you are thinking about a person or a situation. How you feel about yourself comes from your thoughts. When our feelings are triggered, we often react, rather than calmly respond. To be calm enough to respond and not react, we have to choose intentionally and regulate our attitudes and thoughts. Our repeated actions, either positive or negative, create habits. Our habits are what ultimately create the results and outcomes we experience. Coaches using a transformational coaching approach help people increase awareness of the link between the results and outcomes they are experiencing and the underlying beliefs, thoughts, and feelings that got them there. Coaches help people practice changing habits of thought by facilitating self-awareness. Their role as a coach can be critical in helping others take responsibility for their perceptions, thoughts, feelings, actions, and outcomes in their lives. Using universal and targeted facilitation tools can result in profound insights and significant changes in thought habits. For this to happen, coaches need to invest the time and energy to model this reflective journey. The following story offers a concrete example of how transformational coaching can lead to lasting change.

Hot Tip

The key to being self-empowered, rather than a victim of your circumstances, is being responsible for your perceptions.

I was recently coaching a coach who was overcommitting her time and was chronically stressed about her to-do list because she felt that the most important thing was to accomplish goals and outcomes. Through reflection, she began to unravel that the cause of this stress and pressure was internal self-expectations that she should be perfect and do things "right." As she examined her attitude, she realized this was a voice in her head she had learned, and that she had unconsciously inherited these beliefs from her father and his expectations of her as a child. With reflection, she identified that she did not want to operate from these internal expectations anymore; they were not serving her. She actually wanted to be kinder and more patient, value the progress she was making, allow herself to make mistakes, and not let fear—which was adding so much stress—run her life. These were big goals for her, but she was willing to do the work to change her beliefs, thoughts, and habits. It was worth the journey to get there.

She saw how her current beliefs were affecting her coaching. Unintentionally, she pressured the providers to complete their compliance requirements and goals because she felt this pressure in herself. She thought achieving the goal of completing an Environmental Rating Scale (ERS) assessment was the primary focus, and she would often stage a classroom (set up the environment without input from the provider) to ensure the provider would get a good score on the assessment. Her intent was to help, but the actual result was not what she wanted. Actually, the outcome had become so important to her that she ignored, overlooked, and was frustrated by the fact that the provider often rearranged the classroom back to how it had been previously. After the ERS observation was complete, the provider had not learned the reasons for making the changes and how they affected the children, and she did not understand or value the environmental changes the coach had made. Through reflection, this coach recognized that both she and the provider were approaching this as if "passing the test" was the goal, missing the whole idea of fostering CQI. This coach had a huge insight by recognizing that her own internal values—doing things perfectly and getting everything done on time by any means—had influenced the strategies she was using with providers. Once she identified this, she set new goals to be more intentional and patient with herself and her coachees. She decided to take more time teaching the principles behind the environment setup, being less directive with the provider, and encouraging the provider to share her thoughts and reasons for her current practices. The coach created an action plan for herself to use more open-ended questions. She wanted to help the provider examine her current practices in relation to the impact they have on the children and the indicators on the ERS, and then to let the provider lead in deciding what to work on. This coach was willing, even if it was uncomfortable for her, to practice self-regulation in her own habits to refrain from staging the environment and trying to fix the problem for the provider. Here's what her action plan included:

- Practice breathing when she felt physical symptoms of pressure.

- Be patient by preaching to herself, "Real change takes time."

- Engage the provider through reflective inquiry, even though it might take a little longer than just doing it for her.

Intentional Transformational Coaching Strategies

As this coach's coach, I could have simply told her that staging the provider's environment was not very effective and would not accomplish the ultimate goal of the provider learning best practices. But my telling her this likely would not have convinced this coach, as she had years of experience doing this and had thought it was more important to get higher assessment scores. In addition, since her perspective was that she was actually helping, she may have felt judged had I challenged her, and this could have damaged our trust relationship. Rather, by inquiring and being authentically curious about why she chose the fixing-and-staging strategy and by asking why she felt so pressured to meet the compliance goals, I gave her the opportunity to unravel and reframe this for herself. I was her thinking partner, asking her questions she typically did not ask herself. Through her own discovery process, she became willing to make some big, uncomfortable changes. Using a transactional coaching approach—just focusing on goals and actions— would not have led to this same outcome. It required a transformational approach, exploring and examining the underlying thoughts and values that her actions were anchored in. With her new insight, she took the necessary actions, beyond what I might have hoped was possible. I never cease to be amazed by how much change can occur, and how quickly, when the learner is intrinsically motivated, which happens through reflective practices. It is typical for people to shift their goals as they gain a deeper understanding of what they really want. With time and practice, this coach will learn to ask herself the hard questions more often and not get caught in living the unexamined life.

Reflection in Action

Take time to reflect on what you learned in this chapter and its impact on and value for you.

_____

_____

_____

_____

Key messages:

- Cultivate habits of reflection
- Promote habits of reflection
- The power of reflection
- Practice reflection for response-able coaching
- Reflection expands perspective
- Explore frames of reference to expand awareness
- Perception is power

Objective: What are key words or phrases, quotes, concepts, stories, activities, or ideas that stand out or stick for you personally?

_____

_____

Reflective: What part of this feels affirming or inspiring? What aspect feels like a stretch or might be challenging for you?

_____

_____

Interpretive: What was most relevant and meaningful for you? How does this information affect your work or coaching practices?

_____

_____

Decisional: What implications does this have for your actions in the future? What are you most committed to putting into action?

_____

_____

GROOMER Framework for Change Model

The GROOMER Framework for Change is a mental model that helps coaches facilitate the change process. It is like a map to guide coaches through the process of facilitating a person's ability to foster critical thinking, reflective practices, and problem solving by examining the necessary component areas for them to achieve sustainable change. This model can be used both with an individual and at the program level—with teams, programs, agencies, or systems—to facilitate and groom conscious change to promote CQI. Coaches, consultants, administrators, or community leaders who work with early childhood teachers or administrators can all benefit from this model. The framework is a practice-based, inquiry-based, and transformational coaching approach.

It supports coaches in learning an approach to facilitate change, transferring principles and strategies to practical and successful implementation in the field. This transference of principles to practice is anchored in the transformational approach to coaching, rather than a transactional approach. This means coaches first learn to identify and build on their own strengths, explore and shift their attitudes and behaviors, and increase their self-awareness and metacognition. Doing this work is the foundation on which coaches improve their own professional practices to broaden, deepen, and help them master intentional, differentiated, and conscious coaching practices. They are then able to more consciously and skillfully model the same transformational approach for the people they support, their coachees, to self-reflect.

The framework is a universal coaching approach focused on the seven components of the change process. It helps inform coaches on what to discuss and explore with learners about any kind of problem, topic, or professional practice to achieve any goal or desired result. It is a systematic approach for helping people think critically about what they are doing, examine whether their actions are working successfully, and take initiative toward making improvements. The framework is actually not a content-based expert model, but a universal approach to facilitate a coachee's change process, growth, and learning around any topic. This model is not dependent on or bound by any specific kind of topic, curriculum, or focus. It

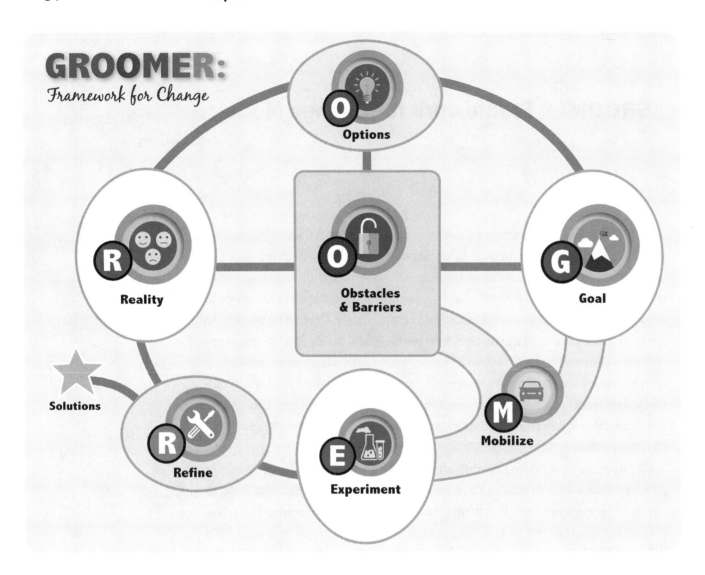

GROOMER:
Framework for Change

Options

O

Reality — R

Obstacles & Barriers — O

Goal — G

Solutions

Refine — R

Experiment — E

Mobilize — M

provides a structural container for supporting change and is easily aligned with many content- or fidelity-based coaching models. It supports people in learning *how* to change and become problem solvers, rather than focusing only on *what* to change and solving only specific problems or topics, which is common in a transactional coaching approach.

The acronym *GROOMER* is offered as an easy way to remember the seven components of the Framework for Change Model. Coaches help groom people to intentionally change and grow. The GROOMER acronym stands for the seven components of ensuring change: Goals, Reality, Options, Obstacles, Motivation, Experiment, and Refine. This chapter describes each component and outlines how the coach can benefit from, use, and apply the GROOMER Framework. The components of this model *do not* need to be followed in any sequential order, though it is important to explore each component at some point in the coaching process to achieve sustainable change. Coaches follow wherever a coachee starts, helping them flesh out additional considerations they may need to think critically about. I refer to this as a "followership" approach where the coach follows the lead of the coachee, rather than a leadership approach where the coach leads and directs the sequence of inquiry and actions. There is no right entry point or sequence for a coaching conversation. Each person might start a conversation at a different point. Some might start by discussing the details of a problem they are facing (Obstacle) or sharing about what's currently happening (Reality), and some might start with a very clear goal and desired outcome (Goal). Coaches follow their lead and help their coachees reflect on each of the components at some point in the process. Rarely does this happen at once; it typically occurs over time.

Coaches help people build on their strengths, and they individualize the exploration of the components based on coachees' needs, current focus, and interests. Coaches also facilitate their coachees' exploration of other GROOMER components they may not be as skillful or experienced in contemplating and addressing on their own. It takes time to reflect, brainstorm, set goals, create action plans, practice, and refine one's habits to achieve lasting change. It's the coach's role to accompany and facilitate the coachee's reflective journey. The framework can serve as a change-process map to intentionally ensure that a person is aware of, has considered, and has reflected on each of the components that are typically necessary to successfully learn, achieve goals, and attain sustainable, lasting change.

> *"Coaching, you see, is not telling people what to do; it's giving them a chance to examine what they are doing in the light of their intentions."*
> —*James Flaherty,* Coaching: Evoking Excellence in Others

This chapter provides a brief description of what needs to be explored and considered for each of the GROOMER components. Later chapters will describe specific tools for facilitating reflection. Each GROOMER component description will close with an excerpt from a coaching conversation I had with a coachee, Debra—a woman who was experiencing stress while preparing for a special event at work. These conversations illustrate how I facilitated her reflection about each component area of the framework over two sessions. Note that the coaching conversations didn't follow the sequence of GROOMER components as they are presented here and so may seem a little disjointed. For example, we had a conversation about obstacles before discussing goals. This is a realistic example of how a coaching conversation can start at any point and follow an individual's unique sequence of exploration.

Goals

Identify desired outcomes and indicators of results:

1. Determine what the coachee wants to happen.
2. Describe concrete and specific goals.
3. Give time frames for goals.
4. Include criteria for success (how they know they have achieved their goal).
5. Identify how to quantitatively or qualitatively measure outcomes.

Knowing where a person wants to go is critical for a successful journey. Coaches need to understand the specific goals, outcomes, or results an individual wants to achieve. For some, this is easy and clear; for others, visualizing and verbalizing concrete, measurable goals is very difficult, and they may need support. You can simply ask, "What are your desired outcomes?" or "What do you want?" or "What do you hope for?" Sometimes the softer language can be helpful because people might not think in terms of goals and outcomes. The question could be framed as "What do you want to happen?" An important part of clarifying goals is to specify the *criteria for success*—that is, how the coachee will know when they have achieved their goal or had success. It might be something that is easy to measure, such as getting a higher rating on an assessment. But when it's something harder to define, such as learning how to handle a child's challenging behavior or how to stay calm during tough conversations, it might take deeper facilitation. That's what it means to specify the criteria of success.

Measurable indicators, as mentioned, can be qualitative or quantitative. Qualitative indicators of behavior change might be body language, a reframed thought or verbal message, or specific actions and their frequency. Napoleon Hill said, "A dream is a goal with a deadline." Without a clear focus and a deadline, it is easy to procrastinate, to waffle around being vague, or to just hope to achieve the desired outcome somehow. So the first step to success is to convert a dream and desire into a SMART goal:

Specific: What exactly will you accomplish? Describe this concretely and give specific examples.

Measurable: How will you know when you have reached this goal, using qualitative and/or quantitative indicators or collecting specific data?

Attainable: Is achieving this goal realistic with effort and commitment? Do you have the resources to achieve this goal? If not, how will you get them?

Relevant: Why is this goal significant to your life or profession?

Time-based: When will you achieve this goal? What is the time frame?

In the introduction to the *SELF Journal* goal-setting planner, Cathryn Lavery and Allen Brouwer (2017) write, "In the 1960s, University of Maryland psychologist Edwin Locke and University of Toronto psychologist Gary Latham, discovered that goal setting is one of the easiest ways to increase motivation and enhance performance. . . . Locke's research revealed the nature of the relationship between how difficult and specific a goal was and people's performance on that goal. He discovered that specific yet difficult goals led to better task performance, rather than vague or easy goals." In other words, it's good to get out of your comfort zone.

Yoga Journal reports, "Recent research from Dominican University shows that people who write up and send action commitments to a friend (along with weekly updates) usually achieve significantly more of their goals than those who keep their written goals to themselves" (Levine 2015). Coaches act as partners to coachees by helping them set specific goals and create action plans to get there, then witnessing and documenting their progress. In this way, the coach acts as an accountability partner, increasing the odds that coachees will achieve their goals.

SAMPLE QUESTIONS: GOALS

Here are the types of questions that promote reflection and inquiry into this component of the change process:

- What do you want to happen?

- Where do you want to end up?

- What kind of outcome or result would you like?

- What would it look like if you got to where you want to be or achieved the results you want?

- How would you know if you reached that place and accomplished those results?

- What are some specific indicators of success?

SAMPLE COACHING SESSIONS: GOALS

First Session

CONSTANT: "What would you like to work on?"

DEBRA: "I am really stressed and feeling like I have a lot to do. I have that internal pressure feeling."

CONSTANT: "If you were able to find some strategies to reduce your stress, what is it that you would like to happen while you are preparing for this special event?"

DEBRA: "To be calm and stay focused on my priorities and to feel okay about only focusing on those tasks during this time."

CONSTANT: "So your goal is to stay calm when in a stressful situation, like preparing for this special event, and to prioritize your tasks, not try to do everything, and feel okay about limiting your focus?"

DEBRA: "Yes."

Second Session

CONSTANT: "Do you feel you are accomplishing your goal of being calm and focused on your priorities?"

DEBRA: "No, not really. I do remember more often now—it's a little better—but I still forget, and the stress seems more, not less. I also want to keep my health practices in place so I don't feel even more stressed."

CONSTANT: "What would maintaining your health practices look like?"

DEBRA: "I would be getting enough sleep, taking time to eat and not work at the same time, and sticking to my exercise schedule."

CONSTANT: "How often do you want to exercise, and how much sleep is enough?"

DEBRA: "Walking with my friend at least three times a week. I need seven to eight hours of sleep to really be productive and not get sick. And I want to take lunch breaks and not work while I'm eating."

Reality

Clarify the current situation, issue, or problem:

1. Determine what's happening currently or what happened in the past.
2. Identify the current context, situation, or circumstance.
3. Clarify what's currently working.
4. Identify strengths, benefits, advantages, and successes.
5. Determine what's currently *not* working or is an area of need.
6. Work to recognize limitations, disadvantages, concerns, and failed attempts.

Coaches need to be sure to talk about the reality of the current situation. It's important to look at both what's working and what's not working. This can also be framed as a person's strengths and weaknesses, or what's easy or hard. The point is to help the person accurately summarize the current situation. Describing their current reality helps people frame where they are in relation to where they want to go. This is important to do at the start of an inquiry or journey; it can also be helpful to revisit this component later during the change process to reflect about progress and document updates. Ask for concrete and specific examples so you are both clear. Sometimes the coachee has not really reflected on what's happening that may be affecting the situation or goal. This type of conversation fosters critical thinking skills as the coachee analyzes and evaluates the current situation.

SAMPLE QUESTIONS: REALITY

Here are the types of questions that promote reflection and inquiry into this component of the change process and identify the current situation:

- What's currently working or not working?

- What are some strengths you can leverage or weak areas that need development in this situation?

- What are some influences affecting this situation positively or negatively?

- What's one positive or negative example of what you're talking about?

- How long has this been working? What's contributed to this success?

- When did this start or stop working? What happened?

SAMPLE COACHING SESSIONS: REALITY

First Session

CONSTANT: "Is there something specific you are feeling stressed about, or is it generic?"

DEBRA: "I'm feeling stressed about a big event our team is planning that's coming up in about a month."

CONSTANT: "What aspect of the upcoming event is stressful?"

DEBRA: "I normally have a lot to do, and now with this special project, I have an overwhelming number of things to do. It's hard to stay focused on what tasks are most important. I am trying to do everything, and it's too much. I am not able to prioritize."

Second Session

CONSTANT: "How has it been going getting ready for the event and staying focused and calm?"

DEBRA: "The event is in about a week, so I'm pretty much going crazy. My practice of using sticky notes to remind myself of my priorities has helped a little. When I look at them, I'll stop and focus, then reframe my thinking."

CONSTANT: "Say more about how the stick-note strategy helped and if there was something about it that didn't work so well."

DEBRA: "Seeing these notes did cause me to think back to our conversation about what I want to happen. But in between those times, I slipped back into trying to do everything. I have also been letting go of all my 'systems,' including good self-care habits, and that's making me less focused, more stressed, and tired."

CONSTANT: "What specific habits did you have that you have let go of?"

DEBRA: "I haven't been sleeping enough and am not exercising, so I have less energy when I need to have more."

Options

Use expansive, innovative thinking and brainstorm multiple possibilities:

1. Brainstorm possible ideas, plans, and solutions for any of the components during the change reflection process—goals, actions, solutions, obstacles, or ways to refine a practice.
2. Generate several possibilities, at least three, to extend considerations beyond obvious and undemanding solutions.

Brainstorming helps generate new ideas that cultivate problem solving and critical thinking. This is a time to say "Yes!" to any and all ideas, no matter how outrageous they might seem. "Options thinking" fosters and develops creative, out-of-the-box thinking. Editing or refining will come later, either when a coachee finally decides what direction to choose or during refinement. This is a time to allow messy, fantastical, creative, and inclusive thinking. Brainstorming embraces not knowing answers and increasing what might seem like unreasonable options. This is a valuable aspect of the process of learning to change and is a formal aspect of the design thinking process. It nurtures and cultivates open-mindedness and possibility thinking. Encouraging a minimum of three possibilities avoids the tendency of assuming the first idea is the best, or making an either/or or right/wrong judgment when only two ideas are suggested. Planning will be more successful if a coachee has engaged in in-depth possibility thinking before committing to specific actions. For some, this is a very exciting, easy, and creative process. For others, not knowing, not having answers, or not understanding how something can be accomplished is quite difficult and can even feel nearly life threatening emotionally. They will need to feel safe in order to experiment. It's critical that coaches are safe partners for their coachees to help them stretch and explore this skill. The Options component has many benefits, including the following:

- To help people learn brainstorming skills and generate many options, especially ways to solve complex problems.

- To cultivate the essential quality to tolerate and embrace change gracefully.

- To cultivate the ability to step beyond our own frame of reference, understand other ways of thinking, and expand limiting attitudes.

- To model creative possibility thinking and brainstorming skills for both teachers and children.

Coaches, of course, first need to practice and embrace this skill and these attitudes themselves to lay a strong foundation for problem solving, invention, critical thinking, and creativity. Those of us who work with young children ourselves, or with the adults who work with children, want to nurture and expand their ability to create and imagine options and possibilities for ideas, goals, and solutions. It is the foundational mind-set and skill set to learn about how to change that increases the odds of having successful outcomes that will stick over time. The GROOMER Framework for Change has an iterative aspect. Again, this framework approach is not necessarily linear or sequential. People fluidly revisit or repeat ideas or components. The Options aspect of the change process fosters the kind of flexible, open-minded, creative thinking that will support a person in being responsive to and willing to follow this nonlinear, fluid, investigative, inquiry-based approach at any time in the change process.

SAMPLE QUESTIONS: OPTIONS

Here are the types of questions that promote reflection and inquiry into this component of the change process:

- Can you think of a few possibilities to close the gap between where you are now and where you want to be?

- How many ways do you think there might be to accomplish that?

- That's a good idea, what's another?

- What are at least three different ways you could look at or approach this?

- Do you know of any other perspectives or options, perhaps what your colleagues have tried?

- Let's consider a range of possibilities. What would be the best option, the average option, and the worst option?

SAMPLE COACHING SESSIONS: OPTIONS

First Session

CONSTANT: "What are some things you might consider changing or doing to reduce your stress, stay calm, and keep focused on your priorities? You don't have to commit to anything now; let's just explore options."

DEBRA: "Most of the time, I use sticky notes to remind myself of my priorities. I haven't been doing that lately. I could try that. I also need to remind myself that it's okay to just focus on my priorities and not try to do everything all at once. Some things will have to wait until after the event. Maybe I need a separate sticky note with that reminder."

CONSTANT: "It's great to start with strategies that have worked for you in the past. Sounds like using sticky notes is a possible strategy to help you focus on priorities and give yourself permission to limit your tasks for now."

Second Session

CONSTANT: "Do you need a reminder that the choice you are making is between (a) unsupportive habits that allow you to feel you are doing everything you can, or (b) positive habits that support your well-being, even if you're stressed? Or did this conversation shift a perception enough for you to remember?"

DEBRA: "Well, I feel like I've gotten clearer about something, but reminders are always helpful. I get caught up in things, and then I can't remember it."

CONSTANT: "Again, it sounds like you have awareness. You can see the value of staying conscious of this choice, but you have to be reminded about it frequently to keep making that choice."

DEBRA: "Yes."

CONSTANT: "Once you're reminded, you seem to make good choices. So the last strategy to put up sticky notes and use verbal reminders has at least partially worked. Is there anything else that would help you remember the choice you're making?"

DEBRA: "Well, it does help me to talk with a friend. Maybe it would help if our team just reminded each other of our priorities and helped hold each other accountable for our self-care."

CONSTANT: "So you want to check in with your colleagues more than just at your morning meeting?"

DEBRA: "Yes, and I could tell a colleague when I'm going to take twenty minutes to go sit in another room and eat my lunch. This would remind myself of my commitment to my goal to maintain my well-being. Maybe I could also have an exercise buddy."

CONSTANT: "Those are great options. We can take a look in a moment at which of these actions you might want to do and include in your action plan."

Obstacles

Clarify challenges and barriers that are causing a gap or blocking progress:

1. Clarify whether the obstacle is an external challenge, which may be negotiable or not. Identify internally rooted obstacles, which are typically a person's perception and interpretations.
2. Help the coachee focus on where they have the most control. Typically this will be internal barriers, as we have no control over other people and little control over external demands and expectations of the workplace, and unforeseen life circumstances.

The most common kinds of obstacles and challenges that people face in the workplace can be described by the acronym *AAMESS*. If these obstacles are not addressed, we typically have "a mess" to deal with—hence, AAMESS. Following is a brief summary of these obstacles. These obstacles are common when dealing with any kind of change and when fostering lasting, sustainable change, regardless of the industry, type of problem, or a person's job. See chapter 7 for more detailed descriptions and practical strategies to bust these barriers.

Awareness: lack of self- or interpersonal awareness

Attitudes: limiting attitudes or negative perspectives

Motivation: lack of, unclear, or conflicting motivations

Emotions: lack of self-regulation, strong emotional trigger reactions, fear, blame, anger, or unworthiness

Stress: Feelings of anxiety, pressure, and being overwhelmed, often caused by overload—too much to do and too little time

Skills: Lacking knowledge or mastery of needed skills

This component addresses the gap between where coachees are and where they want to be. Usually that gap includes a challenge or barrier the person is facing. Part of a coach's job is to help people identify and address the current challenges and barriers to accomplishing their goals.

SAMPLE QUESTIONS: OBSTACLES

Here are the types of questions that promote reflection and inquiry into this component of the change process:

- What's the most glaring thing in your way?

- If something were going to stop you, what would it be?

- Do you think that's an internal or external barrier?

- Does that challenge or obstacle feel approachable or not? If not, why?

- What obstacles or challenges have stopped you in the past?

- Are your current habits or behaviors working for you? Are they getting you the outcomes you want? If not, why not?

SAMPLE COACHING SESSIONS: OBSTACLES

First Session

DEBRA: "With this special project on my plate, I have an overwhelming number of things to do."

CONSTANT: "Are you clear what the priorities are, or do you need to figure that out?"

DEBRA: "I know what the priorities are, but it's hard to stay focused on them with everything I'm trying to do."

CONSTANT: "So it sounds like your priorities are clear but your overwhelming feelings cause you to lose focus while preparing for your big event. Could you name the top five priorities?"

DEBRA: "Yes, I know what they are. I just forget and lose sight
of them."

Second Session

DEBRA: "My internal pressure has increased with the upcoming
deadline. I fall back into my bad habits of trying to do everything when I'm not seeing my sticky-note reminders. I still
lose my focus."

CONSTANT: "Have you found strategies in the past that helped when
you had demanding external pressures, or has it always been
like this?"

DEBRA: "It's always been kind of like this."

CONSTANT: "If you were going to think about the four areas of life—
mental, emotional, physical, and spiritual—is there anything
you're doing that's making this internal pressure worse
or your ability to respond to the situation worse? Or is there
anything from those areas that you think could help you
calm down and refocus?"

DEBRA: "When there are deadlines like this, I don't exercise, I get
less sleep, I eat while I'm working. I have spent time in my
life changing these habits and having healthier self-care routines, but as this event gets closer, I kind of slack off in those
areas, which makes me feel tired and more stressed."

CONSTANT: "Do you recognize, then, that the choices you make
about self-care have a fairly high price?"

DEBRA: "Yes, they do have a high price. And it's not just while I'm
working on the deadline; it takes time to recover after each
achievement."

CONSTANT: "So you're noticing that while this fix seems reasonable
in the short term, it isn't easy to get back into your healthy
routines. The pressures are still the same, and this choice has
long-term side effects."

DEBRA: "Yes."

CONSTANT: "I want to ask you to do a Cost/Payoff Reflection. You
must get something, or think you get something, out of that
unsupportive choice. What benefit do you get out of reducing self-care? Because if you didn't get a benefit, whether it's
actual or not, you probably wouldn't do it."

DEBRA: "I get a feeling that I'm doing everything I can to meet my
deadlines."

CONSTANT: "So you pay the high price to get the feeling that you are doing everything you can. Is it more important to have that feeling than it is to maintain your self-care?"

DEBRA: "When you put it that way, no, I don't want to pay that kind of price!"

CONSTANT: "Right! This is about the impact of making compounded choices—choices repeated over time. If you're not aware of the impact your choices have, it contributes to repeating poor choices or a negative habit. Would it help if you could reframe your choices around sleeping, exercising, or eating so you could see the effects of your choice? (1) I get to not sleep enough, eat while working, and not exercise and feel tired and stressed—but I do get to have the feeling that I'm doing everything I can. Or (2) I can choose to maintain my health and make time for self-care practices, even if I'm feeling really pressured."

DEBRA: "Yes, I think so."

Mobilize

Make action plans both to achieve goals and to deal with obstacles:

1. Create goal plans to achieve desired outcomes. Focus on *how* to proceed to get to the desired result.
2. Create targeted action plans to address specific obstacles and barriers to implementing goal plans or achieving desired results. Focus on *how* to bust the barrier or overcome the challenge to ultimately be successful.

This Mobilize component is focused on identifying and clarifying the next steps to achieve both goals and actions necessary to overcome obstacles and barriers. There are two kinds of action plans:

Goal Action Planning: This is a strategic plan addressing how to achieve a goal.

Targeted Action Planning: A targeted action plan is a concrete, strategic plan to bust a specific barrier or obstacle to achieve a goal or implement a Goal Action Plan.

Often people need both kinds of plans. Usually the Targeted Action Plan will need attention before the Goal Action Plan can be implemented successfully. Sometimes a specific obstacle might not show up for a while, only becoming apparent after the coachee has made mistakes or has difficulty trying to achieve their initial Goal Plans. Both Goal and Targeted Action Plans need to include specific, concrete actions or changes a coachee will make within committed time frames. Use any helpful planning approach and individualize for the coachee's needs. (Several planning and documentation form options are described in chapter 8, Documentation, and the actual reproducible forms are available on the website. Chapter 7, Tools for Busting Obstacles and Barriers, also includes practical tools that can be used to support people in overcoming each of the specific AAMESS obstacles.

Caution: Some people want to rush into creating Goal Action Plans without reflecting about their current Reality and Obstacles, or brainstorming Options. Premature action plans often need to be revisited and modified to be successful. While a lot of learning comes from trying ideas and not being successful, just a little focused reflection in these other components can offer a preventive strategy to strengthen action plans. Try to facilitate conversations about those other components before a coachee finalizes any action plans.

SAMPLE QUESTIONS: MOBILIZE

Here are the types of questions that promote reflection and inquiry into this component of the change process:

- What is one small step that could get you started?

- What is one bad habit or behavior you could replace with a positive one?

- What is one simple action or task you could do daily that, over time, could make a difference in overcoming that obstacle?

- Do you think your plan will work? Why or why not?

- How could you reframe that attitude or philosophy to achieve a more positive outcome?

- What can you do daily to remind yourself of your goals and plans?

SAMPLE COACHING SESSIONS: MOBILIZE

First Session

CONSTANT: "Is there a way you could remind yourself or keep your
    top five priorities in focus?"

DEBRA: "I use sticky notes a lot to stay focused. I could write the five
    priorities on a sticky note and keep it on my desk or computer."

CONSTANT: "Does that seem like a viable strategy to try?"

DEBRA: "Yeah! I can try that."

CONSTANT: "When will you start?"

DEBRA: "Tomorrow!"

Second Session

CONSTANT: "So you will continue using your sticky notes, which do work, but they are not a frequent enough reminder. And you have added targeted actions to help you overcome some new obstacles. To help you remember your priorities on a more regular basis, you decided to call your colleagues throughout the day as necessary to reinforce your priorities and to stay focused. When will you start using this strategy?"

DEBRA: "Tomorrow."

CONSTANT: "You also identified other actions to correct negative choices about your well-being that add pressure and undermine your resilience. You decided to ask a colleague to be your accountability partner, someone with whom you can share your intention about taking a lunch break each day. When will you start this?"

DEBRA: "I can also start that tomorrow."

CONSTANT: "You are committing to getting seven to eight hours of sleep a night. When will you start this?"

DEBRA: "I will start that next Monday. I'll turn off my computer and start to wind down by eight o'clock at night and be in bed by ten o'clock."

CONSTANT: "You said you were going to get an exercise buddy. Do you have one?"

DEBRA: "I haven't found someone to work out with every day, but I do have a friend I occasionally walk with. But sometimes I cancel our walk during times like this—when I'm busy and stressed. I could ask my friend to not let me back out of our walks."

CONSTANT: "Okay. What's the code word your friend should say to remind you that you promised not to cancel?"

DEBRA: "She could just say something like, 'No. We've got to walk.'"

CONSTANT: "How often will you walk, and when will you start this committed action?"

DEBRA: "I want to walk at least three times a week. I will call my friend tonight and try to set up a schedule."

CONSTANT: "These are additional targeted actions to help you increase the frequency of reminding yourself to refocus on your priorities, to reframe your self-talk, and to support your well-being habits. Do you think keeping your health practices in place will be doable, possible, and realistic?"

DEBRA: "Yes, I can do this. If I'm not doing my best with my health, and I'm not feeling well, then sticky notes and things like that don't make much difference. But if I'm feeling like I have energy, then those kinds of strategies can be pretty helpful."

Experiment

Take action, implement plans, try out ideas, and learn from trial and error:

1. Reflect to actually learn from trial and error, mistakes, failures, and successes.
2. Document what's working, what's not working, and the coachee's current progress.
3. Tweak current actions and make ongoing modifications while continuing to implement and practice positive habits.
4. Collect data and document experiences, assessment results, and new information learned or practices implemented.

Implementing an action plan or idea, which follows the Mobilize component, often takes time and repetition. Plans rarely work the first time out of the gate. The process of taking action, implementing plans, trying ideas, and learning from trial and error is all part of the Experiment component of the change process. This is often where creative design and learning occur. This is where the real action takes place to make deep, sustainable changes. And this is the component that can be a little messy, difficult, and uncomfortable; people often stop prematurely or give up. In this Experiment component, coaches play an essential role in helping coachees tolerate the discomfort of learning and making mistakes, and to stick with it so they are able to manifest change in behaviors, attitudes, and skills. Reflection must occur to really learn from trial and error, mistakes, failures, and even successes. Evaluating, reviewing, and analyzing what's working and not working, tweaking what the coachee is trying, and eventually making modifications are all part of the change process. During the Experiment component, coaches use both universal and targeted facilitation tools to help people reflect, describe, and observe their progress. They also facilitate reflective analysis of progress and evaluation to discover, reveal, and clarify any barriers or obstacles. The results from this facilitation could be to make mild modifications or to make a new, more focused Targeted Plan to bust specific obstacles that have become apparent. During coaching conversations, coaches provide support by documenting not only the milestones of progress, but also the coachee's approach to the change process itself.

Conversations during the Experiment component typically include observations, feedback, and reflection on what's happening in terms of their intentions, practices being implemented, success regarding desired outcomes, and how a person's attitude, values, and thinking are influencing those outcomes. This is also a ripe opportunity to examine the link between a person's goals and actions with the actual implementation of ideas, strategies, and behaviors. In addition, it's important to assess the actual or perceived impact of those practices on the children or other adults. I call this the Intent–Impact Assessment. Sometimes what we intend is not aligned with what actually happens. For example, a director might give a teacher feedback about an interaction with a parent, thinking the feedback was matter-of-fact and to the point. But from the teacher's perspective, the feedback was harsh, did not have any context, and was upsetting. The action did not produce the intended impact, and further reflection may be needed on the director's part on how to refine her feedback style. It is often during the Experiment component when coaches are tempted to fix the problem, give advice, or share their good ideas, with the intention of helping. While it's tempting to solve the problem for a coachee, this action's impact is often to interfere with the coachee's own initiative and learning process. Since the GROOMER Framework is an iterative process, coaches might have to encourage the coachee to go back to the Obstacles component and reconsider what's blocking any progress. Often this can't be anticipated before plans or ideas are tested. Once what's in the way is clarified, the coach can help the coachee make a new Targeted Plan. This work often involves helping coachees think about how their mind-set, thoughts, and feelings are affecting how they're tackling new or challenging ideas, behaviors, or strategies. Metacognition (thinking about one's thinking), or self-regulated learning, is the process of taking control of and evaluating one's own learning and behavior. This is the heart and goal of coaching—to help people really see and understand how they learn so they can solve problems and make the changes they desire and need. Documentation of a coachee's progress is really important, as it makes their learning visible. A person can journal about what's happening, what's working, what's not, and why. Coaches can provide support by discussing and documenting what a coachee reports and describes, or what the coach observed or heard during coaching meetings. It's important to capture not only a coachee's milestones of progress but also their approach and responses to the change process. This can help them see what's happening in terms of outcomes and also the impact of their mind-set, and how their thinking, values, and attitudes are influencing those outcomes. This is the core of what facilitation looks like in the Experiment component of implementation.

A coach's own attitudes about mistakes, failures, and successes are critically important because they influence how the coach facilitates and either consciously responds to or unconsciously reacts to other people's behaviors and actions. The parallel learning process here is particularly important—coaches must do their own reflection and metacognitive learning.

SAMPLE QUESTIONS: EXPERIMENT

Here are the types of questions that promote reflection and inquiry into this component of the change process:

- What resources do you need to implement or continue this?

- What mild adjustments have you made while experimenting and trying this?

- What mistakes and failures have you been experiencing? What are you learning from them?

- What successes have you been experiencing? What is contributing to this success?

- What are you discovering by doing this?

- What did you anticipate? What has been a huge surprise?

SAMPLE COACHING SESSION: EXPERIMENT

CONSTANT: "Did using the sticky-note strategy remind you to limit your focus to the priorities that you and your team identified?"

DEBRA: "Yeah, it helped a little bit, but I still fell back into my habit of trying to accomplish all three pages of tasks I had. I felt pretty stressed out by the whole thing."

CONSTANT: "When you say that it helped some, how did it help? What did it change, or what kind of help did it provide?"

DEBRA: "When I would see the note, I'd stop for a moment and go, 'Oh yeah, that's right! I do have this priority.' I would talk to myself differently, which would override the other message, at least temporarily. It helped me keep my work activities focused on the priorities."

CONSTANT: "It's really great that the sticky notes helped you. It sounds like it helped you shift your perspective and reframe your attitude."

DEBRA: "Yes."

CONSTANT: "When you did shift that negative self-talk, how long would that last for?"

DEBRA: "About five or ten minutes."

CONSTANT: "Since we last met, you had only a few five or ten minutes here and there?"

DEBRA: "No, several a day. But there was a lot of time in between those when I would forget."

CONSTANT: "Several times a day is better than having it only once and then forgetting the rest of the day. It sounds like that technique helped remind you. You're actually going through the three steps of stopping, refocusing, shifting your self-talk, and changing your activity engagement. That's pretty successful. It sounds like the strategy works but not often enough, and you might need to refine your strategy or add others."

DEBRA: "Yeah, I didn't realize it really was working and it is the frequency that needs attention."

CONSTANT: "Is there anything else happening?"

DEBRA: "Well, when there are approaching deadlines and I feel this pressure, the systems kind of just go away."

CONSTANT: "What kind of systems go away?"

DEBRA: "My self-care practices of getting enough sleep, exercising, and pausing work to eat. I just plow through."

CONSTANT: "Do you feel like your new targeted actions will cover the next gap, or do you feel like you need to think about other strategies as well?"

DEBRA: "I think this will be very helpful. If I can just put enough attention on it so I take care of my health and do my work projects, that would be a big thing."

CONSTANT: "Your plan is to continue using your sticky-note reminders and to add some targeted strategies. You will increase the frequency of reminding yourself about your priorities by talking to your colleagues more often during the day. You are also adding several strategies to maintain your self-care routines so you don't make those unsupportive choices that compromise your health and add pressure. For example, you are going to talk to a colleague about your intentions and say something like, 'I am promising to take a lunch break without working every day.' In addition, you are going to go to bed by ten o'clock at night and walk with a friend at least three times a week."

DEBRA: "Yeah, I can do those things for sure. I think it will really help."

Refine

Examine and analyze lessons from the Experiment component and make modifications and refinements to find solutions, better practices, clarify next steps, or deepen the reflection to go through another iteration of reflection using the GROOMER Framework:

1. Evaluate, review, compare and contrast, and analyze what has been learned based on the data and results gathered so far.
2. Analyze and evaluate data to discern possible next actions, choices, and modifications.
3. Examine data and current results in context of desired results and the criteria for success. Choose solutions, narrow down options, or clarify next actions. This may mean clarifying and refining a specific solution or deepening another iteration of the reflection process to clarify next steps.

The Refine component of change involves taking the lessons from the Experiment component and making modifications and refinements to ensure success, find a solution, or clarify what more needs to be done. This process is about narrowing down options based on data, information, and experience. During the Refine component, analyzation and evaluation are important tools to help you discern next actions. Help the coachee evaluate data or documentation of both mistakes and successes, as well as progress, and then make choices and changes to achieve what they want to happen. Sometimes a solution is found or a new, beneficial habit is developed that just needs continued practice and maintenance. Sometimes further investigation is needed, a deeper issue reveals itself that needs contemplation, or coachees discover they need to rethink their original plan or their goals. In this case, it's best to go back into another round of inquiry using this same GROOMER model. Completing the whole reflective process of all the components in the GROOMER Framework for Change model would be considered the first iteration of reflection. Because the change process is cyclical and not always linear, it is not uncommon to go through additional

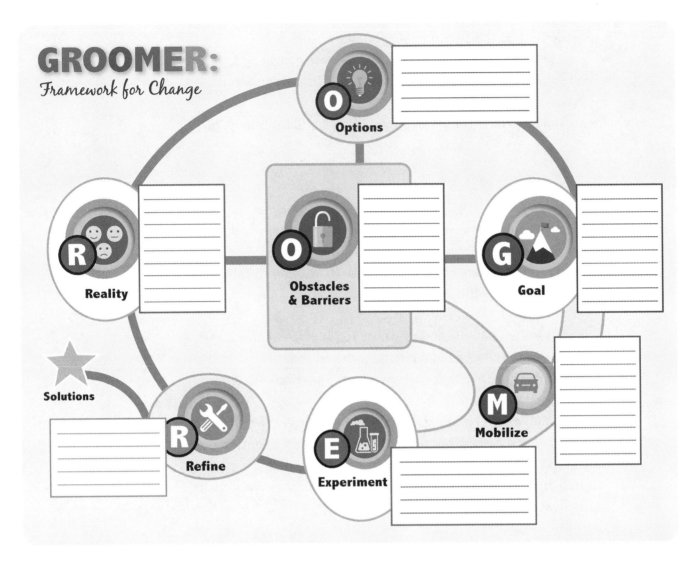

iterations to find actions, behaviors, and habits that cause sustainable and lasting change. This iterative process also supports the nature of continuous quality improvement, in which the true goal is to "get better at getting better," and that is an ongoing process. Yet it is important to document, witness, and acknowledge any milestones of progress and success along the way.

SAMPLE QUESTIONS: REFINE

Here are the types of questions that promote reflection and inquiry into this component of the change process:

- What have you learned from your mistakes and failures? And how are they influencing your next steps?

- What has been a clear success that you definitely want to repeat and continue doing?

- What needs further refinement and a little more attention so you get the outcomes you want?

- How can you now make this a daily habit or practice to sustain this change?

- What adjustments can you make?

- How well do you think your solution will stick? Do you need to deepen the reflection and inquiry process again given this new starting point?

SAMPLE COACHING SESSION: REFINE

CONSTANT: "It sounds like you're trying to build in some accountability for your commitment to reduce your stress, stay calm, and maintain your health and self-care practices even when there is a lot to do at work."

DEBRA: "I have a goal that I want to maintain—exercise, sleep, and eat well while I'm working to get this event done. I'm also trying to stay focused on what we really need to do."

CONSTANT: "One next step is telling your teammates about your goals and desired outcomes while you're trying to meet this deadline. You also want to ask them to be your accountability partners."

The GROOMER Framework for Change Is Fluid and Responsive

The GROOMER coaching model is designed to help coaches facilitate a conversation and reflective inquiry with a learner. Each component focuses on a particular area to think about, and each is important for the learner to consider in order to achieve sustainable change.

This sample coaching conversation with Debra provides a way to examine the natural flow of the conversation and yet see how each of the components were considered. In the first coaching conversation, Debra named an Obstacle—her stress and overwhelm. She then described her current Reality in detail, which helped clarify the challenges she faced. Through facilitation, she determined that her desired outcome or Goal was to stay calm and focused on her top priorities, even in the face of challenging circumstances like the upcoming event. She brainstormed some possible Options for achieving her goals based on successful past strategies. With further discussion, she decided to try the sticky-note strategy to help remind her of her priorities. This conversation reveals the fluid nature of the GROOMER model. A coach can follow the lead of the learner while also ensuring the coachee thoughtfully considers all the components. This conversation did not start with a Goal but rather with an Obstacle. As I coached Debra, we discussed her Reality and what was not working in more detail; I helped her consider her Goals and what she wanted to happen; I also encouraged her to brainstorm possible strategy Options; and finally, I helped her focus to decide on an action to Mobilize her energy. Not contemplating the Experiment and Refine components until a little later in the coaching process is common. In our second conversation, Debra revisited the same components, deepening her reflection. She also talked about how it was going implementing her action (Experiment), additional actions she saw for dealing with new Obstacles, and ways to further Refine her original strategy. Documenting outcomes and progress is done not just to help coaches remember what has been discussed, but also to help make coachees' learning visible to them so they can witness their own growth, progress, and change along their journey. The following is a completed sample of the GROOMER Framework for Change Documentation Form, which is a summary of my notes from our coaching sessions. Chapter 8, Documentation, reviews how to use this form, and others, in more detail.

Coaches can use several different universal and targeted facilitation strategies (see chapters 5 and 6) to help people change. Typically, coaching centers around helping coachees set goals, create action plans, learn *how* to reflect and think about their thinking, and examine their underlying beliefs, thoughts, feelings, and resulting behaviors. A summary of the sample questions for each of the GROOMER components is available on the website. The GROOMER Framework for Change is a mental model for coaches to facilitate this reflection by ensuring all perspectives of the seven components are deliberated to foster sustainable change.

Coach: Constant   Coachee: Debra   Date: First and second coaching session

GOALS: WHERE I WANT TO BE—DESIRED RESULTS/OUTCOMES

First session goal:

to be calm and stay focused on the priority tasks and to feel okay about that

Second session goal:

keep my health practices in place so poor health doesn't compound the pressured situation

REALITY: WHERE I AM NOW—CURRENT PRACTICES

First session

I'm really stressed and feeling like I have a ton to do—a lot of that feeling of internal pressure.

Second session

Writing things down on a sticky note was helpful. It did cause me to think back to our conversation about what I want to happen.

The event is coming up in about a week, so the external deadlines are more intense and I have many things to do. I'm pretty much going crazy and saying to myself that the sticky notes didn't help. But I know that the sticky notes did remind me to prioritize. When I saw them, I'd reframe my thinking. They helped me stay focused on priorities for five to ten minutes, and this happened three to four times a day. In between those times, I slipped back into trying to do everything.

I am also letting go of all my systems, including self-care habits, and that's making me less focused, more stressed, and tired.

OPTIONS: POSSIBLE IDEAS ON HOW TO CLOSE THE GAP

First session

Use sticky notes to stay focused and remind myself of my top five priorities. Don't try to do everything all at once—some things will have to wait until after the event.

Second session

Talk to colleagues throughout the day about staying focused on priorities. Tell my colleagues that "I'm going to take twenty minutes to go sit in another room and have lunch" to remind myself of my commitment to my goal to maintain my well-being and to be held accountable.

Get more sleep.

Have an exercise buddy.

OBSTACLES: BARRIERS AND CHALLENGES
First session

I am trying to do everything at once, am not prioritizing, and am feeling overwhelmed.

Second session

My internal pressure has increased with the upcoming deadline, and in between using the sticky notes, I fall back into my bad habits of trying to do everything and not prioritizing. The reminders are not frequent enough to keep me on track.

I'm feeling more stressed, tired, and pressured, not only because there's a lot to do but because I've dropped out of my self-care habits:
I am working a lot, working through lunch, or eating while working.
I am not sleeping as much as I need to.
I am not exercising, so I have less energy when I need to have more.

I am able to see the high cost of letting go of self-care, but I'm doing negative behaviors because I get the payoff, which is a feeling that I'm doing everything I can to meet my deadline. But I'm seeing that this feeling isn't worth the price!

MOBILIZE: NEXT STEPS AND PLANS; GOAL PLANS
First session

Use sticky notes to remind myself to focus on my top five priorities and not try to tackle everything all at once.

Second session

Continue to use sticky notes to remind myself of my priorities. Add a sticky note that some tasks will have to wait until after the event, and that's okay.
Increase frequency of priority focus by talking to colleagues repeatedly during the day.

Targeted Plans:

Second session

- Continue to have reminders about what I am choosing to do to achieve my goals—to increase my awareness.

- Talk to coworkers throughout the day about staying focused and prioritized.

- Talk to colleagues and tell them I am taking time to eat lunch and not work—to remind myself of my goal to maintain my well-being and to consciously choose well-being over the short-term feeling that I'm doing a lot by working all the time.

- Call my friend to take a walk at least three days a week, and tell her to remind me not to cancel.

- Go to bed by ten o'clock, and wind down by eight o'clock. Get seven to eight hours of sleep per night.

EXPERIMENT: WHAT'S HAPPENING DURING IMPLEMENTATION

Second session

- I was using sticky notes to remind me that it's okay to focus on just the few priorities, and they did help me shift my negative self-talk and reprioritize at least several times a day. But in between, I lose my awareness, fall back into old patterns of trying to do everything, and then feel really pressured internally. Remembering to remember is still a challenge.

- When I remember, I do actually shift my self-talk, and that helps.

- I realize I have fallen into old, bad habits of dropping my well-being practices (sleeping, eating, exercising) when I'm really stressed, and it's actually making things worse—I'm more stressed and feel more pressure.

REFINE: FINALIZE SOLUTIONS OR MODIFICATIONS TO MAKE

Second session

Call my coworkers to remind each other throughout the day to stay focused and prioritized.

Increase strategies to help me remember to do what I know to do—continue with sticky notes and maintain my well-being practices even in stressful circumstances.

☐☐

REFLECTION ACTIVITY

What aspects of this GROOMER Framework for Change model are new or different from the model you currently use?

_____

_____

In what ways could this model deepen your coaching skills and practices?

_____

_____

☐☐

Reflection in Action

Reflect on what you learned in this chapter and its impact on and value for you.

_____

_____

Key messages:

- The GROOMER Framework for Change Model is a mental model for change agents to help facilitate a learner's change process.
- The seven components of the GROOMER Framework for Change are Goals, Reality, Options, Obstacles, Mobilize, Experiment, and Refine.
- The GROOMER Framework for Change is a fluid and responsive model that does not need to be followed in sequence, but rather is designed to follow the learner's lead.

Objective: What are key words or phrases, quotes, concepts, stories, activities, or ideas that stand out or stick for you personally?

_____

_____

Reflective: What part of this feels affirming or inspiring? What aspect feels like a stretch or might be challenging for you?

_____

_____

Interpretive: What was most relevant and meaningful for you? How does this information affect your work or coaching practices?

_____

_____

Decisional: What implications does this have for your actions in the future? What are you most committed to putting into action?

_____

_____

The Continuum of Professional Development Facilitation Strategies

The Professional Development Facilitation Strategies Continuum is used by change agents, including coaches, to facilitate the professional development, overall learning, and change of individuals working to gain proficiency and mastery in their lives and professional practices, and to achieve goals and desired results that are sustainable. Viewing these strategies as actions, behaviors, or verbs, not as individual roles, job descriptions, or nouns, is important. If your job title is *coach*, *consultant*, or *specialist*, you will likely need to use many, if not all, of these strategies to be effective with different individuals at different stages of their professional development. While this book is specifically for coaches, scaffolding the growth of individuals in a holistic approach requires using additional facilitation strategies besides the tools and skills that uniquely define coaching as a strategy. Clarifying and differentiating these strategies is important, and so is being proficient and intentional about choosing the most effective strategy for the individual learner. Each strategy is like a unique tool in a builder's toolbox, and one is not better than another. Yet each tool has a particular use and purpose. In much the same way, all these facilitation strategies are needed to meet individual needs.

The Continuum of Professional Development Facilitation Strategies

Teaching/ Tutoring	Consulting/TA	Mentoring	Coaching

Differentiating Facilitation Strategies

A coach will likely need to use all the facilitation strategies on this continuum at one point or another. It is important not to overuse one particular strategy just because it's most comfortable or because it's the default when you are stressed. This chapter will explore the unique definition and purpose of each strategy, how these strategies are different from one another,

The Continuum of Professional Development Facilitation Strategies

	Teaching/Tutoring	Consulting/Technical Assistance	Mentoring	Coaching
Role and Responsibility	• Assess learning needs • Facilitate learning of knowledge, skills, and competencies • Plan curriculum and scope of content • Use engaging adult learning principles	• Identify problems • Help solve/fix specific problems • Increase skills • Give suggestions/ solutions/advice • Provide resources, referrals	• Share personal experience and offer support • Typically be with less-experienced person • Share workplace or professional protocols and procedures • Share workplace culture and perspectives	• Expand habits of self-reflection • Promote self-awareness and mindful intentionality • Foster critical thinking skills • Normalize change as process • Facilitate change • Promote self-improvement and self-modification to maximize their own performance
Nature of Relationship	• Authority • Content expert • Evaluates learner's competency and knowledge acquisition	• Position of nondecision-making authority (may be formal or informal) • Content expertise and experience • Adviser and problem solver	• Nonauthority • Adviser • Expert • More experienced buddy	• Nonauthority • Content/field expertise or experience *not* necessary • Thinking partner and guide

	Teaching/Tutoring	Consulting/Technical Assistance	Mentoring	Coaching
Styles of Delivery	• Choose pedagogical/ teaching methods • Provide resources • Use a variety of media/ technology • Create and evaluates practicum/projects	• Observation • Feedback • Demonstration/ modeling • Advice/suggestions • Provides resources	• Dialogue • Conversation • Suggestions • Storytelling	• Dialogue • Paraphrase • Inquiry • Reframing • Summarizing • Role playing • Goal setting and action planning • Accountability partner • Documentation of progress and outcomes
Purpose	• Help others acquire knowledge, understanding, and competencies • Assess learner needs and competencies	• Solve problems • Identify and make recommendations for specific issue/problem	• Foster professionalism • Increase leadership • Provide emotional and/or professional encouragement	• Foster problem-solving skills • Facilitate sustainable change in performance and goal achievement • Encourage self-reflection and analysis • Provide partnership to think, plan, and implement new thoughts, actions, and habits

when to choose and use a particular strategy, and under what circumstances one strategy might be more effective than another. Mastering the use of each strategy will take learning, practice, tolerating making mistakes, and being reflective about your own practices. When coaches see that their practices are not effective, they need to be able to quickly modify their behaviors, pick another strategy, and "slide" either to the right or left on the continuum to meet the coachee's needs.

Comparing and Differentiating Professional Development Facilitation Strategies

The chart on the previous pages summarizes the unique focus for each professional development facilitation strategy to help coaches choose the most effective strategy to individualize. This chart and the following descriptions are offered to increase your understanding of and ability to differentiate these as strategies, rather than presented as job descriptions. Although a person may have a specific job description like *consultant* or *coach*, they will in practice use most of these strategies.

TEACHING/TUTORING

When helping coachees achieve goals and improve practices, coaches may find the coachee lacks a specific skill or the understanding or knowledge needed to succeed. Or perhaps they need to comply with new or unfamiliar professional standards, guidelines, or performance criteria. In such situations, teaching or tutoring may be the best strategy. Teaching can happen in both formal and informal settings, with large or small groups or with individuals, which I call tutoring. Whether it is a part of their job description or not, most coaches will at one time or another need to provide tutoring or informal training. Relying only on a coaching-specific strategy when a coachee needs to acquire a new skill or knowledge simply won't work. For example, let's say you are working with a teacher who only knows how to set up activity tables (in which the teacher puts one material on a table for all the children to do), and this is the only way she offers activities. This person is having some discipline issues because the children are not engaged and are perhaps bored. When talking with the teacher, you learn she does not know how to set up and stock a learning center (an area where many different materials and activities are permanently presented for children to select for themselves). This is an excellent example of when it is appropriate to use a teaching strategy—in this case, tutoring the coachee in what a learning center is and how to set up one. Using coaching-specific strategies here wouldn't be effective because reflection alone isn't what's needed. Educating and teaching the actual skill or knowledge must happen first for the coachee to implement this new practice. Many early childhood educators receive only a minimum level of formal education about child development, teaching strategies, classroom management, environmental design, and other information needed to be proficient in working with young children. This is why supporting teachers in the classroom often requires using the facilitation strategy of teaching/tutoring.

Coaches should be thoughtful about the teaching method, or pedagogy, they use when working with adults. Consider the learner's background knowledge, environment, and goals as well as standardized curricula as determined by the relevant authority. Remember, there is a difference between teaching and ensuring that learning occurs. Using a didactic approach of lecturing to impart the information is often not the most effective teaching method. An experiential, Socratic, or constructivist approach—methods that use discussion and questioning, projects, or the implementation of ideas from the coachee's own experience—might be a better choice. In short, be intentional about which teaching methods you use, use engaging adult-learning principles, and, ideally, model the teaching strategies you would like the educators to use with children.

In the field of early childhood, many providers need to complete quality assessment tools, such as the Environmental Rating Scale (ERS), Classroom Assessment Scoring System (CLASS), Ages & Stages Questionnaire (ASQ), or the Desired Results Developmental Profile (DRDP). Recently, many coaches have found themselves teaching to the test. This can mean providing training on the basics of the assessment, how to complete an assessment tool, or how to understand the results. Yet all too often providers are not offered instruction or experiential learning opportunities to connect this information to how the indicators affect continuous quality improvement and the children. Both coaches and providers might view these assessments as hoops to jump through for compliance from funders or stakeholder agencies and often choose a directive teaching approach with this material. However, this is an area where it's advisable to consider using a more experiential and constructivist approach, which might benefit the providers—and the children they work with. While the content covered in the assessments, or any curricula that is taught, may be mandatory, it still makes sense to be intentional about the strategies you use to help providers understand the information and then implement it in their work. This is not automatic. Moving from theory to practice takes effort and often requires a combination of facilitation strategies. This is one reason that coaching has become such a strong trend in both business and education, because teaching information alone does not change people's behaviors. Research from Bruce Joyce and Beverly Showers (2002) revealed that when on-the-job coaching was added to professional development training, large gains were seen in trainees' knowledge, ability to demonstrate the skills, and the use of the new skills in the classroom. The following table presents a summary of a meta-analysis of the effects of training and coaching on teachers' implementation.

Professional Development (Training) and Ongoing Coaching and Administrative Support

Components of training	Percent of learners who will know how to do it	Percent of learners who will be able to do it	Percent of learners who will do it consistently in daily practice
Presentation/lecture	10	5	0
Presenter modeling	30	20	0
Participant practice feedback	60	60	5
Ongoing coaching and admin support	95	95	95

This research reinforces the power of using coaching as a strategy to significantly increase performance and guide educators through the change process of implementing best practices learned in the many trainings offered and required of early childhood educators.

CONSULTING/TECHNICAL ASSISTANCE (TA)

Consulting or offering technical assistance (TA) helps people identify and solve specific problems by giving expert advice. I use the terms *consulting* and *TA* synonymously in this book. Consultants often use assessments to identify problems or needs and then find the resolution to issues of specific concern. The problem could be at the organizational program level, related to staff, or related to children and families; either way, consulting is aimed particularly at identifying and clarifying problems. When coaches use consulting or TA, they often offer ideas, suggest solutions, provide resources, give referrals, give advice, and observe the coachee's environment, behaviors, professional practices, and interactions. Then they give feedback based on those observations and do demonstrations or model specific practices for a coachee.

These are all important and useful consulting tools to help people learn when they need a more structured and directive approach. Consulting is also useful when a specific problem has already been identified. For example, it can be an excellent strategy when a teacher has a child who is acting out either emotionally or physically. In this situation, a coach using a consulting strategy can provide support to clarify what the child's actual problem is, identify the unmet need underlying the child's behavior, and suggest possible intervention strategies the teacher might use to help the child. The coach might ask what strategies the teacher has already tried (checking in about the current Reality component in the GROOMER Framework), and ask which of the suggested approaches or Options the teacher might want to try. Using consultation strategies, the coach could provide specific suggestions and/or resources on how to proceed and demonstrate some positive guidance interactions. These are just a few examples of the several useful and specific consulting targeted facilitation tools to use with coachees when needed.

MENTORING

Mentors are experienced and trusted advisers. A mentor can be older or younger than the person being mentored but should have a certain area of expertise and typically be more experienced. Mentors can be colleagues in similar professional roles, someone the person admires, a more seasoned teacher or director, or someone the person has learned from, like a teacher, a professor, or an adviser on a specific project. In the field of early childhood education, mentors can be formally provided to new hires to help them learn the procedures and the culture of the workplace. This relationship can be formal or informal. Some people report that their supervisor is like a mentor to them. This would usually be an informal relationship, not part of the supervisor's roles and responsibilities. Mentoring typically doesn't include goal setting, following through on a strategy plan, or holding people accountable. It is more about befriending someone, sharing personal experiences, and helping the person better understand their job responsibilities or professional practices. For example, when one woman became a new teacher at a Head Start program, another teacher informally took her under her wing and helped her learn how to dress professionally, how to fill out the required forms, and how to follow the protocols of the center. This wasn't an assigned role from the director, just a colleague who took it upon herself to show this new employee the ropes, answer questions, and help when she had problems. After observing how helpful and successful this role was to the onboarding process, the program director made this a formal role, and now all new hires in this program receive mentoring. I like the metaphor "taking someone under your wing" to describe the way a mentor helps a person learn to fly themselves. This is the essence of mentoring.

COACHING

Coaching, like the other facilitation strategies, has unique benefits, specific purposes, and distinct advantages in certain situations. As mentioned, coaching is typically a new skill set for most educators in the change agent role in the field, especially in how it is different from both teaching and consulting. The essence of coaching is actually capacity building. Here are some of the goals of coaching:

- Expand a person's skills, behaviors, and mind-set, including dispositions in attitudes, through reflection. Help a person set goals, create action plans, successfully implement new practices, and develop new habits to change and become more successful.

- Increase a person's capacity to learn *how* to change, to become more effective, to shift and reframe limiting perceptions and attitudes, and, ultimately, to change unsuccessful behaviors and implement new practices.

My perspective on coaching differs somewhat from the definition of coaching given in the *Early Childhood Education Professional Development: Training and Technical Assistance Glossary* from NAEYC/NACCRRA. It states,

"You don't have to be an expert in a particular field of endeavor to be an effective coach. I don't teach people anything about golf. All I do is help create awareness and self-responsibility in the person being coached. Their own high awareness is their teacher."
—John Whitmore

"Coaching is a relationship-based process led by an expert with specialized and adult learning knowledge and skills, who often serves in a different professional role than the recipient(s). Coaching is designed to build capacity for specific professional dispositions, skills, and behaviors and is focused on goal-setting and achievement for an individual or group" (2011, 11). My approach to coaching is actually not an expert-based model. I believe it is more important for coaches to have the specific skills and experience to foster self-reflection, self-assessment, and self-modification than it is to be a content expert.

Having such content knowledge does not necessarily provide the foundation for excellence in coaching. Currently in the field of early childhood education, most coaches *do* have content expertise. This is not likely to change, given the range of facilitation strategies that are needed to support educators in particular and that do require expertise in this specific field. But having content expertise does carry some inherent challenges for coaches to be successful. Some coaches with deep content knowledge in the areas they coach have trouble refraining from automatically using more directive approaches like teaching, consulting, and providing technical assistance. They often have to overcome and break these habits and mind-sets to learn and use effective coaching strategies and reflective skills. This shift requires patience and the ability to tolerate the discomfort of learning new habits and letting go of the overuse of strategies like fixing and advising, which may have become strong habits. Yet by doing so, the coach learns self-reflection skills right alongside the coachee. As mentioned in the definition of coaching in the *Early Childhood Education Professional Development* glossary, it is common for a coach to be in a different role than the coachee. It's likely that most people reading this book are in this situation. Typically, a coach is somebody coming from outside the coachee's program. But it is becoming more common for programs to have a designated internal coach as a new role or job description, not unlike a program that might have an internal education coordinator. Other programs have peer coaching models, where educators coach colleagues in similar roles. In short, coaching is unique as a strategy because it is designed to help individuals reflect, identify what's working and what's not, identify what they want, and decide how they want to get there. Goal setting and action planning are also unique to coaching as differentiated from the other facilitation strategies. Coaches often become accountability partners. This does not require an authoritative, heavy-handed approach but is about being a thinking partner to help coachees reflect, examine their actions, and document the status and milestones of their progress. In addition, coaches also help coachees examine whether their actions are actually effective, whether they have encountered new barriers, and whether they need to refine any current practices in order to accomplish their goals.

Coaching is not just about helping someone achieve a goal but about supporting the person's awareness and sustainable growth in attitudes, skills, and knowledge. In support of this, the "Coaching Competencies for Colorado Early Childhood Education" states, "Coaching is a learning process based on a collaborative relationship that is intentionally designed to promote sustainable growth in the necessary attitudes, skills, and knowledge to effectively implement the best practices for the development of young children and their families" (Colorado Coaching Consortium 2009). Another unique aspect of coaching is to help reflect, examine, and often reframe coachees' attitudes in addition to teaching new content skills and knowledge. Examining one's frame of reference—a person's beliefs, thoughts, and feelings and how these affect their behaviors and habits—is foundational to the transformational coaching approach. The coaching strategies and skills coaches need to learn include helping a coachee expand their capacity for self-awareness, helping them become self-responsible for shifting and see different perspectives, and giving them the ability to self-prescribe what they need. The goal is for coachees to be able to identify their own needs and to set goals and design action plans on their own. If coaches want their coachees to take that initiative, they have to *not* provide all the answers, suggestions, and advice all the time, using consulting/TA strategies. To embrace coaching strategies, coaches need to intentionally stop fixing things and slide to the right on the continuum, which is a position of less power and authority. Coaching transfers the power to the learner as often as possible. I find that people learn how to coach more quickly when they actually experience being coached and have these coaching strategies modeled for them. It only makes sense that a professional development program for coaches operates as a parallel learning model so coaches, too, can learn this way—receiving formal education about coaching strategies, tools, and coaching models combined with being coached themselves. Hopefully programs and agencies that have coaches are beginning to reexamine their support structures at a systemic level to prepare and invest in the ongoing development of their coaches, including providing them with individual coaching to help them master their own coaching skills. As research indicates, combining training with coaching is the most effective way to support the coaches to consistently implement desirable skills and practices learned in informal or formal educational settings.

Can Supervisors Be Coaches?
While many supervisors would like to use a variety of facilitation strategies to support their staff, in most cases it is challenging for supervisors to be coaches in the workplace. The authority and power inherent in the supervisor's role—making decisions and exercising authority over others—make it difficult for them to also be effective as formal coaches for an employee. That said, supervisors can use a leadership style that is aligned with a coaching approach, such as reflective supervision, in their work.

Differentiating Consulting and Coaching

The two most confused facilitation strategies are consulting and coaching. Many people collapse them—for good reason. More people are familiar and have experience with consulting and are less familiar and have less personal experience with being coached.

Many coaches are put in jobs with little professional development on specific coaching strategies or skills. Usually they are educators who were promoted based on their content knowledge or skill in their existing positions, but they don't necessarily have experience with or training in how to facilitate and coach others. For example, few of us have had a thinking partner to help us reflect and examine our beliefs and attitudes behind our actions and habits of practice; to help us set goals and make action plans; and to help us reflect along the change process until we get where we want to be. Of all the facilitation strategies on the continuum, learning coaching-specific strategies is usually what needs the most attention. That is why it is the main focus of this book.

The simplest way to differentiate these strategies is to use the following familiar metaphor: Consulting/TA *gives* people fish. Coaching teaches people *how* to fish.

The consulting strategy keeps an eye on the problem and finds solutions—the fish. The job is to identify problems and help people get answers, find solutions, and develop specific skills. When coaches use consulting strategies, they climb right in there with the coachee, link arms, and become a partner in solving the problem. The consulting approach keeps an eye on the person's issue, the problem at hand, and works with the coachee to fix problems and find solutions. They offer their expert knowledge and experience, and they might use a variety of tools to help with the problem, such as observing, giving feedback, modeling behaviors or practices, and/or providing resources. Coaching, on the other hand, is successful when coaches keep their attention on the coachee, not their problem. They watch their coachees and how they think and approach their problem. They witness, inquire, and learn how their coachee is going about solving their own problem and then help them expand these skills—how to fish. They are detached from their coachee's problem rather than involved in the story line or drama. This does not mean they don't care or are not empathetic; it just means they focus on helping their coachees develop their own problem-solving skills rather than providing solutions. The coach is skillful in the protocols of facilitating reflective and critical thinking, and in helping people think and inquire for themselves. This can take more time, but the results are worth the investment. In addition, this models for educators the way we hope they will, in turn, help children become problem solvers rather than doing things for the children. Coaches should model strategies in a parallel process. A coach will do the following:

- encourage coachees to examine their motivation, intent, beliefs, and values

- often reframe what they say or how they act so they can see what they're thinking and shift their perspective

- use summarizing and empowering inquiry to help coachees witness their own thinking process

- analyze and evaluate whether current or chosen solutions are working

- become the coachee's thinking partner—not telling them what they should think or advising on the best practices they should be doing

Transformational coaching helps people move from *what* to think (being concerned about having answers) to *how* to think (learning critical thinking and problem solving) to solve problems and create solutions for themselves. Transactional coaching is the more common approach for those who use teaching and consulting strategies frequently. The coaching strategies presented in this book and on this continuum are more aligned with the transformational approach to coaching, and this approach frequently produces more lasting results.

Purpose of Facilitation Strategies

Understanding the purpose of each facilitation strategy helps coaches determine when to use which strategy. It's like knowing when to use which tool in a tool kit. Knowing the purpose of each tool is essential to facilitate sustainable change and individualize an action plan for each coachee. This knowledge helps coaches make intentional choices about sliding along the continuum to use a specific strategy because it's more appropriate for the learner and more likely to be effective. Identifying the intended purpose can help you choose the most appropriate strategy:

- Teaching and imparting information: Teaching/Tutoring

- Fixing problems and finding solutions: Consulting/TA

- Fostering professionalism and sharing experiences: Mentoring

- Increasing reflecting thinking and problem solving: Coaching

Here are some indicators to help you identify when each strategy might be the most effective one to use:

- Situations where teaching/tutoring can be effective
  - a person lacks the specific knowledge, understanding, or skills needed to perform well, achieve goals, or make necessary changes
  - introducing new workplace or industry compliance information
  - someone needs options or solutions beyond their current education, knowledge, or experience to make informed decisions about how to proceed in planning and implementing changes

- Situations where consulting/TA can be effective
    - o advising a program or individual on needed changes regarding specific concerns or problems, often regarding compliance issues, observations, or assessment results
    - o conducting observations as a tool to provide a "second pair of eyes" from a content-knowledge expert or to help gather information aimed at solving a specific problem or concern
    - o offering feedback, often based on observation or assessment results
    - o providing recommendations, suggestions, and/or advice
    - o offering options and/or resources to learners who lack the content knowledge or experiential understanding to generate solutions, possibilities, or ideas themselves
    - o providing best practices standards or guidelines, content knowledge, or community resources, usually to address a specific problem or situation

- Situations where mentoring can be effective
    - o someone needs a buddy to learn about workplace procedures, culture, or specific endeavors
    - o someone needs an adviser for encouragement and support to build confidence
    - o someone needs a more experienced, nonjudgmental resource person who can answer questions and offer perspective
    - o someone needs additional support to increase their professionalism

- Situations where coaching can be effective
    - o someone needs to expand their personal awareness and self-reflection practices, and examine their frame of reference and perceptions, particularly regarding their choices, behaviors, habits, and professional practices
    - o someone wants to make qualitative and quantitative breakthroughs in performance and results
    - o in conjunction with and after any training and technical assistance to support personalization of implementation to achieve desired results and to maximize training investments
    - o a person continually struggles to sustain lasting results or accomplish goals
    - o training and advice are not making a difference

> o   someone knows what to do but isn't taking action
>
> o   someone is resistant or unmotivated to change
>
> o   someone needs to take initiative, own their personal actions and results, and increase their sense of responsibility

☐ ☐

DEVELOPING STRATEGY DISTINCTION ACTIVITY

Use this activity to reflect, compare, and summarize each facilitation strategy.

What did you learn about facilitation strategies that reinforced what you already knew?

_____

_____

Note anything that surprised you or any conflicting feelings or concerns you have about any of the information you read.

_____

_____

What questions do you have about each strategy or about the use of each strategy?

_____

_____

_____

Which feels like your strongest facilitation strategy or the one you use the most? Why?

_____

_____

Which feels like your least developed facilitation strategy or the one you rarely use? Why?

_____

_____

☐ ☐

Sliding along the Continuum

Coaching will not be the best facilitation strategy for every situation. The goal of this book is to help coaches develop the specific skill of coaching alongside the other facilitation strategies so they can choose which strategy to use for each set of circumstances. This means you will want to intentionally slide along the continuum, from the right to the left and back again, as needed. Being able to differentiate between these strategies is core to this conscious decision-making process.

As a coach, you not only need to choose which strategy to use and when but also be able to effectively deliver and facilitate the coachee's learning. Several factors influence which facilitation strategy to choose. Coaches need to employ the following skills:

- individualize their approach for each learner's strengths and needs

- be self-aware of their own strengths and challenging habits

- be mindful of how the power and authority inherent in different facilitation strategies can affect the learner

Sliding along the Continuum of Facilitation Strategies

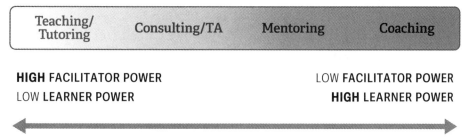

Take note that the coach using the facilitation strategies on the left end of the continuum has *high* power in interactions with the learner—the coach has more power than the learner—and the learner has *low* power in the relationship. The opposite is true on the right side of the continuum. Here the coach has *low* power in the interactions with the learner, and the learner has *high* power. This becomes especially important when coaches want their coachees to take more initiative, or they notice their coachees are becoming too dependent on their suggestions and advice. In this case, you need to change your strategies and slide further to the right to transfer more power to the learner. You need to change your behavior and interaction strategies first if you hope to see different results in the coachee's actions.

MEET INDIVIDUAL NEEDS OF THE LEARNER

It's important for coaches to treat each person individually and to avoid the habit of using the same strategy with everyone. Coaches individualize their coaching by intentionally modifying and adjusting their facilitation strategies. Coaches need to consider a variety of factors as they individualize their coaching. You'll naturally learn some of this information over the course of working with people. To gain other insights, you may conduct a needs assessment, either formal or informal. For example, when I start working with someone, I typically try to identify the person's strengths, interests and passions, areas of competency, favorite teaching topics or centers, and the learning styles or dominant type of multiple intelligences. Identifying limiting or negative beliefs and attitudes can be very important to building a genuine relationship with the learner. Other areas to clarify to individualize your approach include the coachee's frame of reference, education background, and professional experience. In addition, in the course of working with each person, coaches should inquire and learn about their coachees' risk and change tolerance, influential factors in their workplace, their level of personal awareness, and their content-based knowledge in the field. When I am coaching coaches, I may have them complete the self-evaluation checklist from the Colorado Coaching Competencies to get a sense of how they view their competencies or areas where they need support. This can be foundational for setting professional development goals with the coach.

In the course of coaching, a coach will likely need to slide along the continuum of facilitation strategies to individualize and meet the coachee's needs. When coaches begin to master facilitation skills, they might slide along the continuum and use several strategies in one sixty-minute session. In general, when working with adults, I recommend starting with the lightest intervention (coaching) and only slide to the left as tighter scaffolding and support are needed. Often this is the opposite of our natural tendency, especially when a coach has a background in working with young children. With children, educators often start with a heavy scaffolding approach and only back up and use a lighter support or intervention strategy as mastery is demonstrated.

If I work with somebody who needs to gain more skills or knowledge, I might slide to the left on the continuum toward training or consulting to provide more information and teaching, and then slide back to the right on the continuum as soon as possible. Sliding along the continuum isn't something coaches do in a formulated way. It's something done in a uniquely responsive way according to the given needs of the person being coached. There is an art and subtlety to sliding along the Continuum of Professional

Development Facilitation Strategies, which takes practice and active reflection and analysis to master.

It would also be inaccurate to think that experienced teachers need less coaching than new teachers. Experience doesn't always equate effectiveness in all areas. It simply depends on what their next learning goal is or if they need motivation to make changes. Individualizing for the person, the setting, the content, and the context is important.

BE SELF-AWARE AS A COACH

As mentioned earlier, coaches must become reflective and expand their own self-awareness if they are to facilitate change and learning in others. Talking the talk and walking the walk—practicing the same reflective habits you want to develop in learners—is part of the parallel process that effective coaching demands. When it comes to understanding the unique focus and purpose of each strategy on the continuum and knowing how and when to use each, coaches should be aware of their own strengths and challenging habits. Sometimes strengths can unconsciously lead coaches to overuse a familiar or favorite facilitation strategy. In this way, a strength can become a bias.

While most early childhood professionals have personal experience with and know how to teach or provide technical assistance and consulting, their personal experience with coaching may be limited. New coaches are typically more aware of what they don't know and are either eager and open to learn what's needed or feel embarrassed, thinking they "should" know already and judging themselves critically. More-experienced coaches may not understand the distinction between consulting and coaching and don't realize they are actually consulting most of the time. They may lean toward control and leading rather than shifting their focus and inquiry to the coachee's perspective and transferring power to the coachee. They may have developed some habits that can take concerted effort to break, like telling or convincing people what their goals should be, fixing their problems as a first intervention strategy, or teaching to the test.

> Individuals (coaches) who have previous experience as teachers tend to rely on or fall back into a directive mode when:
>
> - They are challenged by a particular situation,
> - When their coaching skills are not yet fully developed,

- When they feel the need to prove what they know, or
- When they are trying to reassure themselves that they are being helpful to the coachee (Stober and Grant 2006)

□□

REFLECTION ACTIVITY

Recall a time when you as a coach fell back into a directive mode. What caused you to do this? What was the result or outcome?

_____

_____

_____

In the future, how could you handle a similar situation, in which it is challenging not to fall back into using a directive mode? List a few actions or strategies you could use. You might add these to your Professional Development Action Plan.

_____

_____

_____

_____

_____

□□

BE MINDFUL OF THE IMPACT OF ISSUES OF AUTHORITY AND POWER

Being mindful about how power and authority influence your choices and the effectiveness of your facilitation strategies requires rigorous reflection and practice. Again, starting with a lower-level facilitation strategy is likely to be more effective than being more directive and using high-level intervention strategies too soon. Remember to transfer the power to the coachee as often as possible. Move to the left on the continuum only as needed. Move back to the right, using low facilitation strategies and power as the learner shows an increase in understanding, skill, motivation, problem solving, or critical thinking.

Start with and continue to use low-level facilitation intervention and power when the coachee

- has low or conflicting motivations;

- needs help reframing an attitude or perspective;

- needs help or time to think or to implement ideas; or

- is not experiencing the desired results or outcomes and needs more reflection and self-evaluation.

Caution! When working with very experienced teachers at high levels of performance, coaches might use low power and intervention strategies only, missing specific areas where those teachers may need focused support.

Move to medium-level facilitation intervention and power if the coachee

- is not succeeding at implementing ideas and plans;

- needs additional help to analyze and think critically about the situation; or

- lacks problem-solving skills.

Caution! Coaches often prematurely use medium-level power strategies when they have a lot of content knowledge, experience, advice, and ideas they think will help.

Move to high-level facilitation intervention and power if the coachee

- has limited content knowledge and understanding;

- lacks experience and resources; or

- needs more concrete examples or demonstration.

Caution! Too often coaches start with high-power strategies when they feel pressured by deadlines or to meet compliance regulations—and then they can start to act like authoritarian regulators.

The following table outlines the advantages and disadvantages of the different facilitation strategies. This can help you analyze why an approach may or may not have worked in the past and can help you determine how to thoughtfully choose which strategies to use in the future.

Other considerations with power and authority have to do with cross-cultural, racial, and ethnic diversity, and the cultural dominance of coaches and the people they serve. Be mindful of your own frame of reference, values, and beliefs concerning your role and responsibilities, and your understanding or lack of understanding of the cultural, racial, and ethnic differences of the people you support. In addition, consider how any cross-cultural, racial, and ethnic tensions in the workplace are likely to affect how you support the educators (both directors and teachers) you are coaching.

Advantages and Disadvantages of Facilitation Strategies

	Teaching/ Tutoring	Consulting and Some Coaching	Mentoring and Coaching
Level of Power and Authority	High	Medium	Low
Facilitation and Intervention Strategies	• Providing information • Giving direction and instruction • Offering external rewards	• Problem solving • Modeling and demonstration • Reframing coaching tool • Intent—impact review coaching tool	• Storytelling • Sharing experience • Dialogue/talking informatively • Paraphrasing and reframing • Empowering and clarifying questions • Providing encouragement
Pros	• Immediate action • Increases skill and knowledge • Quick fix	• Solves problems • Engages learner • Begins reflection and analysis	• Demonstrates trust in learner's capacity and ability • Fosters creative and critical thinking • Promotes initiative and leadership
Cons	• Disempowers responsibility • Triggers reactions • Can damage trust • No lasting change in behavior	• Can undermine initiative and create dependency • Time consuming	• Can miss details • Lacks verification • Release time/ coverage to have conversations and dialogue • Time consuming

In what ways can you transfer more power to the coachee?

_____

_____

_____

_____

_____

_____

Pause & Reflect

Becoming clear about the unique benefits of each strategy on the Continuum of Professional Development Facilitation Strategies can improve your effectiveness as a coach. Knowing how and when to use each tool will take practice. The more you reflect on your professional practices and use the GROOMER Framework for Change to document and analyze your own professional goals, actions, and progress, the more you will reinforce these new skills and habits and deepen your ability to coach others to achieve transformational change.

1. Choose *one* of the following scenarios that best matches the type of person you typically coach: directors, teachers, family home providers, or parents.
2. Reflect on which scaffolding strategies you might use in the scenario. Why? What outcome do you want to achieve?
3. What do you want to know more about? What are your questions to foster reflective and critical thinking for yourself about this situation?
4. List questions you might ask the coachee to foster their reflective and critical thinking about their situation.

DIRECTOR SCENARIO

While meeting with your coachee today, she breaks down crying: she's been putting in more than sixty hours per week while developing a grant proposal, trying to hire a cook, and working to balance the budget, yet she feels everybody still wants more from her. Some teachers have complained to the parents that she's never in the classrooms, doesn't support the teaching staff, and is trying to save money by not hiring a cook. She wants you, as her coach, to solve her problems. She tells you, "I don't know what else I can do. Please, please help me! If you can't solve my problems, then no one can! Maybe I should just quit and walk away from it all."

_____

_____

_____

_____

_____

TEACHER SCENARIO

Teacher D works with infants, and you notice that her diaper-changing procedure is not in compliance with state licensing or program standards. You discovered the teacher was unaware of the regulation specifics and what needed to happen. You explained the expected procedure, and she commented that it really isn't practical to do it that way but reluctantly agreed to change her practices. When you next visit, you see she has made the changes as discussed, so you know she has the necessary knowledge about the procedure, but during the next several visits you notice she has reverted back to her old habits.

_____

_____

_____

_____

HOME VISITOR/PARENT SCENARIO

You are on your first visit to a new family. When you walk into the family's home, you notice that their apartment is tightly packed with stuff—piles of toys, knickknacks on the tabletops, objects under the sofa and behind chairs. Mom tries to clear some room for you to sit. She is concerned that her only child, a three-year-old son, always asks for help, doesn't do things for himself, and doesn't really play by himself. Mom says she is a single mom who does not have other support around her.

_____

_____

_____

_____

_____

FAMILY HOME PROVIDER

You have been working with a small family home provider for several months to increase the quality of her program. The program is about to have a Family Child Care Environmental Rating Scale (FCCERS) assessment done. You have been supporting the provider by ensuring she has multicultural and engaging materials for young children and encouraging her to acquire more materials. On a visit, you notice she has several more of these materials and activities available for children. You acknowledge her for adding these appropriate and well-chosen materials. After the FCCERS is completed, you do another site visit and notice that the new materials are no longer available. She tells you she had borrowed them from another provider so she could have them for the assessment, but she has since returned them.

_____

_____

_____

_____

_____

Reflection in Action

Take time to reflect on what you learned in this chapter and its impact on and value for you.

_____

_____

Key messages:

- Learning to differentiate between the unique focuses of each strategy and when to effectively use which strategy is foundational to coach for conscious change.
- Teaching focuses on imparting information, knowledge, and skills.
- Consulting focuses on identifying and helping solve problems.
- Mentoring focuses on fostering professionalism and sharing experience.
- Coaching focuses on expanding capacity to reflect critically and to set goals, make plans, and implement actions.
- Intentionally slide along the continuum of strategies based on the learner's needs.
- Be mindful of issues of power and authority when choosing which strategy to use.

Objective: What are key words or phrases, quotes, concepts, stories, activities, or ideas that stand out or stick for you personally?

_____

_____

Reflective: What part of this feels affirming or inspiring? What aspect feels like a stretch or might be challenging for you?

_____

_____

Interpretive: What was most relevant and meaningful for you? How does this information affect your work or coaching practices?

_____

_____

Decisional: What implications does this have for your actions in the future? What are you most committed to putting into action?

_____

_____

Universal Facilitation Tools

The GROOMER Framework for Change Model is a universal approach for coaches to foster critical and reflective thinking to promote intentional practices and lifelong learning. Coaches can use both universal and targeted facilitation tools to achieve this goal. Universal facilitation tools are basic tools that help people reflect, become more self-aware, make intentional choices, and make data-driven decisions. Coaches rely on these tools as they use the professional development facilitation strategies presented on the continuum in chapter 4. These tools help learners explore the inner landscape of their desired results, their progress, and how they approach continuous improvement and change.

Targeted facilitation tools are those used to achieve a specific aim or to bust through certain obstacles and barriers. These will be discussed in chapter 6.

In this chapter, we'll discuss the six universal facilitation tools:

1. Pausing and Listening
2. Paraphrasing and Validating
3. Empowering and Open-Ended Questioning
4. Reframing and Organizing
5. Data-Driven Investigating and Extending
6. Analyzing and Summarizing

Pausing and Listening

Pausing is a skill that requires intentionality and awareness to effectively practice. I call this "the fine art of knowing when to bite your tongue." This is probably the most important and foundational human communication tool. Until one pauses, listening is not an option. It takes either authentic curiosity or self-regulation to pause long enough to listen to another person. Too often coaches ask good questions but don't actually allow people the time it takes to respond at their pace. A coach may feel uncomfortable with silence or may be preoccupied with their own thoughts or anticipated responses during a conversation, and this can get in the way of true listening. Yet the tool of pausing helps coaches self-regulate their own behaviors of

- talking too much;

- asking too many questions without allowing people time to respond;

- thinking they are supposed to have an answer; and

- falling into the know-it-all mind-set that impedes authentic curiosity, learning, and true listening.

Listening is one of the real gifts you can give another person—to be fully present to them. There are three types of listening: (1) autobiographical listening, (2) objective listening, and (3) empathetic listening. Here are some ways to become a more effective listener:

1. **Decrease autobiographical listening.** Autobiographical listening is an egocentric way of listening. This distracts you from being fully present to another person and from understanding that person's perspective and experience. There are several types of autobiographical listening:

   o "About me" listener-centered listening: In this type of listening, you might find yourself thinking about how the other person's statements relate to you and your experiences.

   o "For me" agenda listening: This type of listening is focused on an agenda or specific outcome. Waiting to hear something specific can often cause impatience or trigger irritated feelings if you don't hear what you are waiting for.

   o "What's it to me?" self-significant listening: This is listening to decide whether what the other person is saying is relevant to you, has significance to you, or has consequences that may affect you. It's a slight variation of both "about me" and "for me" listening.

   o "I know" listening: This is when you listen through the filter of belief that you already know what the speaker is talking about, that you already understand, or that what they are saying is nothing new. Again, this is autobiographical because it implies that the point is your own understanding or knowledge, as opposed to focusing on the other person, learning, and listening with some humility.

   o "Validate me" affirming I'm okay listening: This type of listening is when you validate or affirm yourself through whatever the other person is saying. This occurs when you have a judgmental perspective focused on comparing yourself to others, usually with the purpose of verifying and confirming your self-confidence.

2. **Strengthen objective listening.** Objective listening is "you-centered" listening that focuses on the speaker. Your attention should be fully on the speaker with the intent of understanding their perspective, viewpoint, and feelings.

   o Listen for the speaker's purpose and agenda, what they are trying to convey.

   o Listen from a neutral and unbiased perspective without trying to interpret or assume meaning. If it is unclear what the speaker is trying to convey, paraphrasing their words or asking simple clarifying questions can be useful to stay present.

3. **Master empathetic listening.**

   o Listen with an attitude of inquiry and attend the speaker fully, giving your undivided attention.

   o Listen for the whole message within the larger context of what's being shared.

   o Listen for the intent and meaning, even if the actual words or verbal message are imprecise.

   o Listen for what's not being said, with kindhearted consideration and care.

   o Listen without judging the speaker, communication, or message.

   o Listen with your eyes and focus on nonverbal messages and their connection to the verbal message.

   o Listen with your heart.

> *"Empathetic (from empathy) listening gets inside another person's frame of reference. You look out through it, you see the world the way they see the world, you understand their paradigm. . . . In empathetic listening, you listen with your ears, but you also, and more importantly, listen with your eyes and with your heart."*
> —*Stephen Covey,* The 7 Habits of Highly Effective People

Paraphrasing and Validating

Paraphrasing involves repeating back or restating what somebody has said with the intent of expressing their meaning. A more natural approach is when you use different words that capture their intent, rather than just parroting back what they said word for word. You must be careful not to put words in their mouth or change the meaning of what they intended. Paraphrasing has several purposes, including validating and confirming the message, pacing to promote self-reflection, and shifting conceptual focus.

VALIDATING AND CONFIRMING THE MESSAGE

This is about affirming that you are fully present, listening, and interested. Often called active listening, paraphrasing communicates and verifies that you understand what the person is saying (or you are trying to). If you're lost or unclear, you can say, "I'm not sure what you mean; could you clarify that or say more?" Afterward, paraphrase to be sure you now understand correctly.

When paraphrasing, be careful to avoid adding any personal interpretation or translating the information through your personal filters. Here are some ways to validate and confirm the message:

- What you're saying is . . .

- Let me see if I get this . . .

- In other words . . .

PACING TO PROMOTE SELF-REFLECTION

Paraphrasing can help pace the speaker, especially if they are speaking really quickly. This is often as much for them as for you. If the person is going faster than you can track, paraphrasing can slow the speaker down so you can stay fully present and be sure you are understanding fully. In addition, when people are talking very quickly, they often aren't aware of it and might be speaking faster than they can consciously reflect on what they are saying. Here are some ways to paraphrase to help pace the conversation:

- You're concerned about . . .

- You would like to see . . .

- You are trying to figure out . . .

SHIFTING CONCEPTUAL FOCUS

Paraphrasing can help "catch and return" a person's thinking, giving the speaker an opportunity to witness and gain perspective of their own thinking. Thinking a thought in your head is very different from speaking a thought aloud to another person. As you listen, you can see patterns or themes a speaker might not be aware of. Through paraphrasing you can offer a conceptual context to help the person gain perspective of what they are saying that can add meaning and insight for them. Here are some ways to paraphrase to expand the speaker's conceptual focus:

- So a *value or belief* you hold is . . .

- So a *goal* you have is . . .

- So an *assumption* here is . . .

Empowering and Open-Ended Questioning

The art of inquiry is more than just asking questions. The foundation of inquiry is about having an attitude and demeanor of curiosity and wonder. When a coach asks questions from authentic interest, those questions have a quality that is unique and felt by the other person. Coaches ideally want to inquire from the objective mode of you-oriented listening and engage empathetically, really wanting to know about what's going on with the other person and eager to understand their perspective.

Here are some ways coaches can practice inquiry:

- Be genuinely and authentically curious and interested, inquiring, listening, and understanding more than just the content of the story line.

- Ask open-ended questions (no right answer) that express your curiosity and empathetic wondering.

- Ask clarifying questions so you can better understand.

- Inquire with your attention on the other person.

- Ask questions that help coachees explore their own thinking, perspective, and insights and expand awareness of themselves in relation to the situation. You are inquiring in order to help them discover for themselves, from within, what they need. You are not responsible for finding an answer for them.

- Inquire from multiple perspectives.

- Inquire with an open mind and without agenda, not thinking you know the answer or trying to fix anything. *No advice!* Inquire and follow the coachee's lead; do not ask questions with a demeanor of leading, wanting them to get to something or reach a specific answer.

In short, ask questions to discover how the coachee thinks, what their perspective is, and how they approach problem solving. By being curious about how the coachee operates, a coach can help them get curious about that themselves. The art of asking questions, even of ourselves, can expand our perspective and our metacognition, and it leverages deeper thinking skills in ways that just seeking solutions does not do. Questions foster investigation and discovery. Most people have the answers they need within themselves. They just need help to access them. Inquiries posed as a route of discovery have a different feeling than questions that are answer driven. In the GROOMER model, coaches foster brainstorming thinking in the Options component. Coaches should expand their own ability to be curious about their own lives and professional practices, and inquire whether what they are doing is effective. It's important to cultivate a demeanor of curiosity and deepen your technical inquiry skills of investigating and questioning. You will be a more effective facilitator if you are doing your own learning and skill development in a parallel process. Using open-ended questions means the person asking the question does not know the answer to the question. Be mindful, because not all open-ended questions are empowering. Empowering questions are expansive. They are not leading, nor do they have a tone that is demanding, judgmental, or interrogative and driving toward a desired answer.

EMPOWERING QUESTIONS ARE OPEN-ENDED

Following are some traits of empowering open-ended questions:

- have no right answers
- can't be answered with yes or no
- have an answer you don't already know
- are designed to move the discussion forward
- deepen experience and insights
- promote self-reflection
- help clarify and gain perspective
- allow people to express themselves and explore how they feel, what they want, or what they think and why
- are expansive, open-spirited, and promote possibility thinking
- focus on what the coachee knows and does not know—and how they know it
- explore from different perspectives
- consider time-relevant questions:
  - o past—history (previous experience)
  - o present—current state or situation
  - o future—concerns, fears, hopes, dreams

- investigate assumptions, values, beliefs, feelings, and expectations
- inquire about rationale, perspective, and attitude

EIGHT TYPES OF OPEN-ENDED QUESTIONS

Following are eight types of open-ended questions coaches can use to empower others to reflect:

1. **Clarifying questions** help make clear one's thinking and encourage concrete, specific analytical reflection. You might ask clarifying questions when the coachee uses vague words, pronouns, or thoughts; to identify underlying beliefs or expectations; or to clarify the coachee's rationale:

    o Who is the "them" you are referring to?

    o What exactly does this mean? Are you saying . . . or . . . ?

    o How does this relate to what we have been talking about?

2. **Comparative questions** explore how things, ideas, or behaviors are the same or different:

    o What if you compared . . . and . . . ?

    o What is the difference between . . . and . . . ?

    o What are the strengths and weaknesses of . . . ?

3. **Questioning assumptions** helps coachees explore assumptions and unquestioned beliefs they may have for their reasoning, thinking, behaviors, actions, or habits:

    o What evidence is there to support what you are saying?

    o You seem to be assuming . . .

    o How did you come to this conclusion or interpretation?

4. **Questioning viewpoints and perspectives** helps people explore their own perspectives and recognize that there may be other, equally valid viewpoints:

    o What are some alternative ways of looking at this?

    o Why is . . . necessary?

    o Who benefits from this?

5. **Future or "what if" questions** encourage forecasting, extrapolation, creative or out-of-the-box thinking, or contemplating possible causal relationships:

   o   What do you think would happen if . . . ?
   o   What are possible outcomes if . . . ?
   o   How might that influence or affect . . . ?

6. **Questions about the question** encourage metacognitive reflection on the coachee's own questioning process:

   o   What motivated you to ask that question?
   o   Is this making sense to you? Why or why not?
   o   Is there a question you are not asking or don't want me to ask? Why?

7. **Standby questions** are like kick-starters to keep reflection going or transfer the power to the learner and foster generic reflection:

   o   What else? Say more . . .
   o   Tell me about . . .
   o   Repeat the last two words of the coachee's last statement as a question to encourage them to continue sharing when there is a lull in their speaking and you are not sure they have finished their thought, such as repeating "Your report?" when the person just said, "He really reacted to my report."

8. **Observation-based content or event-specific questions** are questions that might be asked based on observations:

   o   Can you say more about was happening when . . . ?
   o   I saw you do . . . I am wondering how you decided what you were going to do.
   o   What did you think (a child) was trying to do when . . . ?

When you are supporting people with a specific piece of content, initiative, or focus area, you may find it useful to ask specific questions. Remember to frame these as open-ended questions—questions you *do not* know the answer to.

PRACTICE APPLYING EIGHT TYPES OF OPEN-ENDED QUESTIONS

Write open-ended questions that might be relevant to supporting one of your current coachees. Use as many of the eight types of open-ended questions as possible. Ask questions you are genuinely curious about or that will help you learn more about how the coachee thinks, their perspective, or their actions.

_____

_____

_____

_____

_____

GROOMER INQUIRY QUESTIONS

The following sample open-ended questions cultivate reflection in each of the seven components of the GROOMER Framework for Change model when facilitating the change process. These questions were introduced in chapter 3.

Goals

- What do you want to happen?

- What kind of outcome or result would you like?

- What would it look like if you got to where you want to be or achieved the results you want?

- How would you know if you reached that place and accomplished those results?

- What are some specific indicators of success?

Reality

- What's currently working or not working?

- What are some strengths you can leverage or weak areas that need development in this situation?

- What are some influences affecting this situation positively or negatively?

- What's one positive or negative example of what you're talking about?

- How long has this been working? What's contributed to this success?

- When did this stop working? What happened?

Options

- Can you think of a few possibilities to close the gap between where you are and where you want to be?

- How many ways do you think there might be to accomplish that?

- That's a good idea, what's another?

- What are at least three different ways you could look at or approach this?

- Do you know of any other perspectives or options, perhaps what your colleagues have tried?

- Let's consider a range of possibilities. What would be the best option, the average option, and the worst option?

Obstacles

- What's the most glaring thing in your way?

- If something was going to stop you, what would it be?

- Do you think that's an internal or external barrier?

- Does that challenge or obstacle feel approachable or not? If not, why?

- What obstacles or challenges have stopped you in the past?

- How is that habit or behavior working for you? In what ways is that getting you the outcomes you want?

Mobilize

- What is one small step that could get you started?

- What is one bad habit or behavior you could replace with a positive one?

- What is one simple action or task you could do daily that, over time, could make a difference?

- In what ways do you think your plan will work or not? How could you reframe that attitude or philosophy to get a more positive outcome?

- What can you do daily to remind yourself of your goals and plans?

Experiment

- What resources do you need to implement or continue this?

- What mild adjustments have you needed to make while you've been experimenting and implementing this?

- What mistakes and failures have you been experiencing? How are you feeling about them?

- What successes have you been experiencing?

- What are you discovering by doing this?

- What did you anticipate? What has been a huge surprise?

Refine

- What have you learned from your mistakes and failures? How are they influencing your next steps?

- What has been a clear success that you definitely want to repeat and continue doing?

- What needs further refinement and a little more attention so you get the outcomes you want?

- How can you now make this a daily habit or practice to sustain this change?

- What adjustments can you make?

- Do you think your solution will stick, or do you need to deepen the reflection and inquiry process again given this new starting point?

☐☐

THE ART OF INQUIRY QUESTIONING ACTIVITY

Practice the art of inquiry and explore the power of questioning by completing the following activity on a topic you want to more deeply think about and reflect upon. Do not answer any of these questions at this time. Do not focus on finding answers. Instead focus on finding helpful *questions* to expand your thinking on your topic. Just keep writing one question after another to open up your thinking. Let one question lead you to another. Let yourself wonder and inquire with no pressure to find solutions. Look at the situation from different perspectives. Consider the eight different types of empowering questions you might ask.

Focus or Topic Area for Inquiry (name one situation, topic, or problem you want more clarity about):

_____

_____

Write twenty questions you can ask yourself about this situation, focus, or topic area:

1. _____

2. _____

3. _____

4. _____

5. _____

6. _____

7. _____

8. _____

9. _____

10. _____

11. _____

12. _____

13. _____

14. _____

15. _____

16. _____

17. _____

18. _____

19. _____

20. _____

When you think you have run out of questions, push a little further and write down at least five more questions. Notice whether this is uncomfortable or difficult for you or whether the process feels creative and interesting. Next identify two or three of your questions about which you could ask additional, more helpful or deeper questions, or which you could focus on attempting to answer. Take one of those new questions and dive deeper into that specific question and line of inquiry by writing another ten related questions.

1. _____

2. _____

3. _____

4. _____

5. _____

6. _____

7. _____

8. _____

9. _____

10. _____

Reframing and Organizing

Reframing can shine a light on a person's internal landscape of thoughts and feelings and give them a broader perspective—to move from viewing the trees to seeing the forest. When you help your coachees organize their thinking or develop a contextual framework for where they are, they often gain meaning and a sense of the relevance of what they are experiencing. This can also empower the learner to better make informed decisions on their own rather than relying on the coach for advice and suggestions. Here are some ways you can do that:

- Use the GROOMER Framework for Change as a mental model for yourself to help learners reframe their perspective and organize their thinking about their journey and learning process. Share the GROOMER Framework for Change graphic model and make this model transparent for coachees. Show them where they are using the GROOMER "graphic model" to provide a larger perspective of the change process in which they are engaged. For example, you could say the following:
  - "You have been working hard to clarify your *goals*, and there are still several other areas to focus on, also. What component in this GROOMER model feels like the natural next area to consider?"

- Refer to the seven GROOMER components by name to help the coachee identify what they have been talking about or to frame their actions in a large-process context. For example, you could say the following:
  - "You are very clear on what's not working about your current situation. Are you aware of or do you want to explore the *reality* of what is working?"
  - "An *obstacle* you just mentioned that is stopping you from achieving your goal is . . . "
  - "Now that you are clear about what you want to do and the actions you want to take, it's time to implement and move into the *experiment* phase of the process."

- Identify themes and patterns of thought, feelings, behaviors, or habits to help the coachee gain perspective and increase their awareness. When a person can see patterns, it often helps them identify areas where they need to take action and motivates them to change. For example, you could say the following:

o "I notice at the beginning of each coaching session you say, 'I haven't really done anything,' but our conversation reveals you have actually done a lot. It seems there is a pattern here about your perspective of not being successful."

o "I've noticed that you had to reschedule our coaching session the last three times because you forgot I was coming. This seems like a pattern. What is it pointing to or what is the problem that needs attention?"

Reframing can be a helpful tool when people have a limited or negative attitude or view of themselves or a situation. It allows them to view the situation from another vantage point. For example, I was coaching a manager who felt like he never had good ideas, and he was judgmental of himself. During a coaching conversation, he listed numerous recent insights about why his program was experiencing some challenges. I wrote them down. Later I mentioned the insights and good ideas he had. He was completely unaware of what he had said, commenting that he hadn't had any good ideas. I read his ideas back to him, and he was shocked because he hadn't recognized those as "good ideas." He was quiet for a moment and then said, "Those *were* good ideas! What do ya know!" My framing his thoughts as good ideas enabled him to see them from a new perspective. This really started to shift his self-confidence and self-image.

Data-Driven Investigating and Extending

Gathering information and data through the documentation of conversations, implemented actions, observations, or video or audio recordings can help individuals witness their own thinking, behaviors, progress, and achievements. Initial perceptions are not always accurate—sometimes coaches need to help coachees compare their perceptions with any concrete data they have analyzed about their own actions or the actions of children, staff, or families they may be working with. This can help them gain a broader perspective and understanding. Here are some ways to do that:

- Use documentation forms to record goals, actions, progress, time frames, and achievements.

- Select or design forms to meet your program needs, but be sure that whatever you use collects data and information that is needed by all stakeholders—the coachee, coach, program, funders, and so on. One form may not meet all your different needs.

- If you work with a computerized documentation system, select forms for use in the field that will not only support your need to take accurate notes in your reporting system, but will also help you share meaningful information with the coachee or your supervisors.

- Go to www.redleafpress.org/transformationalcoaching for a variety of documentation forms.

I was coaching a program manager who herself supervises several coaches. In our work together, she had created an action plan to meet several different goals. At the beginning of our second coaching conversation, she reported, "I didn't really do anything on my action list. I wasn't very successful." But as we talked and I documented (on the Action Plan and Status Report) the status of each action, it became apparent that she had taken some steps toward most items on her list, even if the action wasn't fully completed. She was progressing step-by-step toward her goal. As she explained what she did on other items, it became clear that certain foundational steps needed to happen before she could complete the whole plan. While she originally said that she had failed in her assignment, my documentation demonstrated her true progress. Now she could acknowledge the work she had done and see ways that she needed to think through her plan in greater detail. We spent the rest of the session identifying what supporting tasks would allow her to complete each specific action. She broke her action plan down into more specific steps and sequential actions. This process helped her learn how to think more critically and thoroughly as well as how to make more detailed action plans.

The need for modification and deeper thinking is quite common during the Experiment component of the GROOMER Framework of Change. Once implementation begins, many things are revealed that need more attention, modifications, resources, or other people to review materials that might affect completion dates—all of which were not anticipated at the outset. This is exactly why the person's actions in the Experiment component need a great deal of facilitation to successfully navigate through the change process. During this component, coaches use both universal and targeted facilitation tools. This is also a good example of why it's important for both coaches and coachees to use documentation and data collection tools. The process of reframing and summarizing using specific data helps people identify their progress rather than focusing only on outcomes or results.

Having concrete data and documentation can also help address any attitude obstacles, such as discouragement or self-judgment. Reflection and analysis of the documented progress can shift the coachee's attitude from feeling like a failure to acknowledging progress and realizing that change is a process that takes time. Collecting and reviewing data can also help clarify actual behaviors when it is easy to estimate habits or actions inaccurately. I was coaching a classroom teacher who was working on asking open-ended questions. She had identified her goal: to ask open-ended questions 75 percent of the time. She was also trying to reduce the use of directive statements and telling children what to do, with a goal of doing this less than 25 percent of the time. After several weeks, she thought she was doing pretty well. I asked her if it would be helpful for me to observe and just make tally marks for each open-ended question she asked and for each directive statement. I spent three hours in her classroom during different kinds of activities and routines. When we reviewed the results together, we were both shocked. She was asking open-ended questions only 40 percent of the time overall. But the more detailed documentation revealed that during circle time and center free-choice time, she was using open-ended questions about 60 percent of the time. During snack, transitions, and outdoor time, she used directive statements nearly 80 percent of the time. The detailed documentation helped this teacher see what was working and what was not. She realized that she had sensed she was doing well because she only thought about circle time and center time. The data supported—and motivated—her to make changes by creating a targeted plan for how she would increase her use of open-ended questions during snack, transitions, and outdoor time. Within a few weeks, she was more successful and achieving her original goal. Practice-based research shows that when teachers collect useful information about children and about their own teaching habits, it can help them inform their practices and better meet children's needs. Coaches not only want to support this kind of professional practice of teachers and providers but also model it themselves by collecting data and documenting their own progress in achieving professional goals.

EXTENDING

Extending is a tool that supports people in stretching a little beyond their comfort zone or thinking from a different perspective. Many times people's thinking or practices are extended during dialogue, through open-ended questions, or when a coachee completes a specific reflection activity, such as the My Frame of Reference activity introduced in chapter 2. To encourage teachers to think of ways to extend or stretch children's curiosity, coaches might brainstorm with them ways to investigate a topic more deeply with children. It's important to model for and interact with teachers in the same investigative and provocative way you want them to use with children. In *Loose Parts*, authors Lisa Daly and Miriam Beloglovsky summarize the benefits children gain when teachers extend children's thinking by simply adding provocative loose parts—interesting materials—to the environment and helping children investigate rather than giving them answers. They write, "When children engage in investigations, they are involved in asking probing questions, collecting data, analyzing the information, and finding meaningful answers to their original questions" (Daly and Beloglovsky 2015, 180). Teachers benefit in the same way when coaches challenge and help them extend their thinking. For example, a coach might encourage a teacher to explore ways to shift from an activity-based approach to a more investigative approach through the use of projects or themes. Using data-driven investigations and providing coaching can support the teacher to do research and learn from trial and error rather than prescribing or teaching a strategy. This both models and strengthens the teacher's own learning in a parallel process. A coach can extend a coachee's thinking or practices by using the following extending tools:

- Use an investigative approach, ask probing questions, and encourage coachees to collect data, analyze the information, and help them find meaningful answers to their own questions.

- Consider using provocative materials, photographs, or videos in coaching conversations with educators, related to the topic they are working on.

- Suggest ways coachees might approach a project to collect data and documentation about either children or their own behaviors to inform their decision-making and prompt new ideas. Help link concrete experiences to abstract theories so educators can better understand what specific teaching practices or adult/child interactions look like. For example, support the teacher in identifying specific behavioral indicators or actions on the CLASS assessment. Then have them gather data and document their own actions that demonstrate those behavioral indicators.

- Provide videos, photographs, or examples of teachers in action or of children's work to spark conversations to explore new ideas.

Extending a coachee's thinking by using some form of documentation or demonstration of work can be very helpful. For example, try videotaping educators and then watching the video with them, allowing educators to share what they observe. Afterward, analyze the relevance of what they are observing as related to whatever professional practice is being explored. Extending might also involve making a provocative suggestion or asking coachees what new idea they could try or a practice they could implement that might feel risky but would be worth the investigation. Part of the learning process is to expand one's risk tolerance. This is highly individualized based on the coachee's current risk tolerance or which stage of change they may be at. Try to determine the level of risk coachees can tolerate and be willing to nudge and encourage them to take the next step without pushing too hard or too far. Through extending or provocative interactions, some limiting attitudes or foundational beliefs may be revealed that might be worth unpacking. Discovering how beliefs and attitudes are affecting the coachee's professional practices and willingness to try new and different practices can be transformational. The following chapters include several targeted facilitation tools that can be used to do this, such as the Cost/Payoff activity (chapter 6) or the E + R = O activity (chapter 7).

Here are some sample questions that deepen data-driven investigation and extending:

- "What data or information do you have that supports your theory or that your idea might be effective?"

- "How do you know that?"

- "What evidence is there that this is true?"

- "How might you document if . . . is actually happening?"

Remember to gather information about the effectiveness of your own coaching strategies and the facilitation tools you used. Then analyze the impact it has on the coachee. Data-driven investigation can be a tool to help coaches becomes researchers about their own coaching practices, which can reframe or extend a coach's use of new coaching strategies. Through using both data and extending, coaches may identify how they might modify a strategy, how to better individualize, and when they might need to slide along the continuum and use another strategy to better support the coachee.

Analyzing and Summarizing

Analyzing is a critical thinking skill that involves examining and reviewing data with the goal of discovering useful information, suggesting conclusions, and supporting data-driven decision-making. Analyzing therefore goes hand in hand with documentation and data collection. Analyzing can happen at any point in the change process, not just in the Refine component, although that is a major purpose of that component. Here are some tips on when and how to use analyzing in your work:

- Analyze what is clear/unclear, known/unknown, and working/not working.

- Assess the experience of implementing ideas and plans, noting what modifications or refinements might be needed.

- Analyze if the coachee's actions support the process of achieving their desired results. Do they need to break down goals or actions into milestones or smaller steps to be more successful?

- Reflect on insights gained and shifts in perspective and how this has affected behaviors, actions, and results.

- Evaluate whether a chosen solution has been found, if continued experimentation is needed, or even if the coachee needs to reenter the GROOMER Framework for another round of investigation and inquiry.

Supporting coaches in analyzing information themselves, making their own decisions, and setting their own course of action is important. For example, instead of using a directive approach to reviewing the results of an assessment by simply telling coachees about the results, encourage them to analyze the information, draw their own conclusions, or identify relevant goals. This allows the coachee to discern for themselves what course of action might be prudent, and it strengthens their motivation and initiative. Or, as previously suggested, use videos of teachers in action and then debrief and discuss what they see. This is another opportunity to help them analyze the effectiveness of their own actions. The GROOMER Feedback Protocol in chapter 6 offers a constructivist approach to giving feedback. It's important to choose universal and targeted tools and facilitation strategies aligned with an educator's analytical skills, confidence, motivation, and readiness for change.

SUMMARIZING

Summarizing is like paraphrasing but with added complexity. Summarizing helps coachees experience and hear their own thinking process externally. It's a way of reflecting back their speaking, thinking, and actions so they can see it with perspective. This promotes awareness, choice, and responsibility. Summarizing is the link between reflection and action. It can occur at any time throughout a conversation or meeting, not just at the end. Here are some helpful tips on summarizing:

- Summarize the sequence of conversations or events to encourage coachees to witness their process.

- Recap where they started, where they are now, and where they are headed, both in each coaching conversation and throughout the coaching relationship. Use the GROOMER graphic model to help the coachee see this visually.

  o "You were very clear on what you wanted to happen, and you had a clear Goal Action Plan that you implemented. During the implementation process, a few barriers and obstacles became apparent, and you then developed several Targeted Action Plans to help overcome those challenges. You have decided your next step is . . . that you want to complete by . . ."

- Inquire and help the coachee clarify next steps, actions, and refinements needed to achieve their desired outcome. For example,

  o "When you started implementing your action plan, you thought it would only take a month. Now you are recognizing this plan needs additional steps, or the endeavor was a little more complicated than you originally anticipated. You are adjusting your time frame accordingly."

  o "You have identified that you need additional resources and more help to successfully reach your goal."

The universal facilitation tools outlined in this chapter can be used as a coach slides to the right and left on the continuum of facilitation strategies. These tools foster reflection, critical thinking, and problem solving to support coachees in achieving their desired results and learning how to change and take initiative toward their own professional development and the continuous quality improvement of their program. The following chapters will offer targeted tools to deal with specific needs, circumstances, and challenges individual coachees may be facing.

Reflection in Action

Take time to reflect on what you learned in this chapter and its impact on and value for you.

_____

_____

Key messages: Universal facilitation tools include the following:

- Pausing and Listening
- Paraphrasing and Validating
- Empowering and Open-Ended Questions
- Reframing and Organizing
- Data-Driven Investigating and Extending
- Analyzing and Summarizing

Objective: What are key words or phrases, quotes, concepts, stories, activities, or ideas that stand out or stick for you personally?

_____

_____

Reflective: What part of this feels affirming or inspiring? What aspect feels like a stretch or might be challenging for you?

_____

_____

Interpretive: What was most relevant and meaningful for you? How does this information affect your work or coaching practices?

_____

_____

Decisional: What implications does this have for your actions in the future? What are you most committed to putting into action?

_____

_____

Targeted Facilitation Tools

This chapter presents targeted facilitation tools—tools designed to help people achieve a specific goal or to bust through certain obstacles and barriers. Each professional development facilitation strategy, as presented on the Professional Development Facilitation Strategies Continuum in chapter 4, uses unique targeted facilitation tools. The following tools that correspond with each of the facilitation strategies offer choices for the coach as they slide along the continuum to the right or left to meet the learner's needs. Some of these tools could be applied to more than one strategy. Most of the detailed descriptions of facilitation tools provided in this chapter are typically used with either the consulting/technical assistance or coaching strategies.

Basic teaching/tutoring facilitation tools are listed in the tool list table as an overview to clarify what adult education tools might include and

Teaching/Tutoring	Consulting/TA	Mentoring	Coaching
Provide information/data	Observe	Engage in dialogue/ conversation	Engage in dialogue/ conversation
Instruct	Model & demonstrate*	Share personal experience	Promote self- awareness & inquiry
Practice	Offer advice & ideas	Support professionalism	Talk informatively/ narrate*
Engage adult learning strategies	Give feedback*	Give feedback	Reframe perspectives
	Provide resources	Reframe	Reflect on intent & impact*
			Set goals & plan action*

*These tools are described in this chapter. The more common techniques, such as dialogue and advice, do not need specific instructions and are not included here.

how they are different from other targeted tools. I did not include detailed descriptions of these teaching/tutoring tools since presenting the extensive teaching approaches required to successfully support individuals is beyond the scope of this book. For more information on how to engage adult learners, refer to my tool kit of adult education instructional strategies, *Engaging Adult Learners Using Multiple Intelligences* (Hine 2014).

Be mindful, self-aware, and intentional in selecting which facilitation tools to use and when, as this can deeply affect your coaching relationship. Ensuring that the coachee feels respected, trusted, empowered, safe, and able to take risks and make mistakes is important. At times a coach may select a facilitation tool that is too directive for what is needed, and coachees may perceive this as the coach being arrogant and having a know-it-all attitude, being judgmental, or showing a lack of trust in them. On the other hand, if a coachee is uncomfortable, lacks skills, or feels lost and you do not offer enough support, it can foster a sense of confusion and undermine your coachee's confidence and trust in the relationship. Make a practice of observing and assessing whether the tool you selected had the intended effect. Experiencing an "intent-impact gap" is not unusual—meaning what you intended to happen is not actually what happened. Noticing this type of gap is part of your own learning process as you discover how to be more intentional in selecting facilitation tools that meet the coachee's needs. Ask the coachee for feedback about the usefulness of specific tools you have used and whether your current approach is helpful or not, and then modify accordingly.

Consulting/Technical Assistance Tools

These tools offer a more directive or tighter scaffolding approach on the continuum.

MODELING

Modeling is a technique to teach and demonstrate specific skills, interactions, or teaching practices for educators. This can become a more powerful and effective tool if coachees understand what they should be specifically watching and observing. I recommend completing the Intentional Modeling Form before any demonstration to plan and clarify your objectives using this tool. This can also help you note specific points coachees should watch for, including whether they should focus only on what the coach is doing or also on how this is affecting children's behaviors or other potential consequences. Be sure to take the time to reflect as you fill out this form before modeling. You can plan this with the coachee based on both the coachee's desires and needs and your objectives. Doing so can help you avoid shooting from the hip so you can give thought to the schedule, any environmental setup, and the materials needed for the modeling exercise. For example, determine the best place for the coachee to sit to fully observe both the coach and the children. Immediately, or soon after, each modeling exercise, debrief and discuss what the coachee observed and learned. In addition, clarify whether there will be adequate coverage of the children so you will have time to have an uninterrupted conversation. Without time to debrief, the use of this tool is not necessarily effective. Consider video recording the modeling session if it is not possible to immediately debrief with the coachee. Then if you have a debrief conversation at a later time, you can both remember what actually happened. The Intentional Modeling Form can help you guide the coachee's focus and debrief after the modeling exercise, and it provides a space for the coachee to take notes. In addition, be sure to let the coachee share observations, offer insights, and ask questions before you provide any instruction, explanation, or comments about specific things the coachee may not have noticed. This is using a less directive and more reflective approach to debriefing after modeling.

Following is an example of a completed Intentional Modeling Form that I gave seminar participants prior to modeling coaching.

"Experience is not the best teacher. It sounds like heresy, but when you think about it, it's reflection on experience that makes it educational."
—George Forman, professor

Sample Intentional Modeling Plan Form

Purpose of modeling session:

For seminar participants to watch a demonstration of coaching in action with a focus on using strategies from the coaching end of the continuum spectrum, and to model how to use the GROOMER Framework for Change model.

Anticipated learner objectives:

- Observe universal facilitation tools: listening, paraphrasing, empowering open-ended questioning, reframing.
- Observe targeted facilitation tools: talking informatively, and others based on the need during the modeling session.
- Observe the use of the GROOMER Framework for Change as a mental model for facilitating a coaching conversation.

Modeling setting (time, materials, environmental considerations, and so on):

Use a microphone, depending on the size of the room.

Place the coachee's chair at an angle so the person is not directly facing the room of observers.

Setup points (what the learner should be observing, intentionally watching for, and so on):

- Which kind of facilitation tools does the coach use?
- Did the coach slide back and forth between strategies on the Continuum of Professional Development Facilitation Strategies?
- Where on the GROOMER Framework did the coachee start the conversation?
- How much does the coach talk and how much does the coachee talk?
- Who came up with any solutions or suggestions?
- Are there any long pauses when neither person is talking? What do you think is happening during any pauses?

Postdebrief notes:

- What did they observe?
- What insights were discovered?
- What questions were there about any of the strategies or reasons I used them? What questions might participants have of the coachee and what the experience was like for them?

Intentional Modeling Form

Purpose of modeling session:

_____

_____

_____

Anticipated learner objectives:

_____

_____

_____

_____

_____

Modeling setting (time, materials, environmental considerations, and so on):

_____

_____

_____

_____

_____

Setup points (what the learner should be observing, intentionally watching for, and paying attention to):

_____

_____

_____

_____

_____

Postdebrief notes:

_____

_____

_____

_____

_____

Hot Tip

Remember, feedback is an offer, not a mandate.

FEEDBACK GUIDELINES

In human interaction, feedback is a process that helps people see the effects of their behavior. The goal is to help people see the results of their actions so they can decide whether a change is needed to get a different result. Feedback given for any other reason is not feedback—it is criticism, judgment, frustration, or an opinion. I consider it courteous and respectful to always ask if the person would like feedback before I give it, even if it's expected in the role of a coach.

Ideally feedback offers an observation or insight that will help people expand their awareness and understanding so they can make a different choice in the future. Here are some tips on giving feedback:

- General feedback
    1. Identify the purpose and clarify your intent for giving feedback. Beware of wanting to be right, pointing out that someone is wrong, or insisting that they need fixing. Don't confuse giving your advice, judgment, and opinion with feedback.
    2. Ask permission to provide feedback. If the coachee declines, stop; to continue would not be feedback nor a particularly effective tool given that circumstance.
    3. Make it timely, as soon as possible after the event.
    4. Focus on the behavior and actions of the person, not on the person. For example, "You have interrupted me four times in this conversation," not "You are very rude."

- Educational feedback
    5. Let the coachee respond to the information you gave before making additional comments. Encourage them to share what they gleaned from your observation. Discover what they noticed and what value it had for them. Notice what they didn't pick up or comment on. This can inform how you provide additional feedback or determine what discussions to have.
    6. Build on the coachee's strengths and what they have been affected by. Deepen the conversation using that information, following their lead.
    7. Start with positive, authentic feedback about what works. Share specific actions that have had beneficial effects to encourage the person to use them more often. This also supports their confidence and self-concept.

8. Focus on the future. Give feedback to help people control their own performance and make informed choices in the future.

9. Create context about why the feedback might be relevant. Discuss the coachee's perspectives and, if you gave any feedback, ask about the relevance of the data you provided or other feedback points that they didn't mention to further inform any other discussions and to ensure they understood your reason for the feedback. For example, "By asking all those open questions of the new teacher, you were able to find out the points that I was concerned about, specifically about their ability to handle departures with several families arriving at once. That was very helpful to me," not "You conducted a good interview."

10. Watch your tone and demeanor; it affects more than the content you share. Keep it simple and speak slowly and calmly. Use a neutral but engaged tone and demeanor.

11. Be prepared to listen empathetically if the other person becomes upset. Listen to the coachee's perspective of the experience with the intent of understanding them, not defending yourself.

12. Be open to receiving feedback yourself. Avoid becoming defensive and needing to give explanations. Use breathing to stay calm and open.

13. Stay focused on the original issue or message. Keep it simple and to the point. Don't add confusion by trying to offer too much information.

14. When giving personal feedback about the impact a person's behavior had on you, report your feelings and the consequences of their behavior and how it affected you. For example, "When you shake your finger at me like that, I feel like a schoolchild again," not "I don't like your arrogant attitude."

- Observational feedback

  15. Use the GROOMER Feedback Protocol following an observation or when providing results of an assessment. This protocol is designed to be a less directive approach aligned with a coaching style to provide feedback. The following visual graphic indicates when the coach speaks and when the coachee speaks. This protocol allows coachees to lead and offer their observations, impressions, and voice before the coach. This can help reinforce that the coach is not an authority with all the answers and that the coachee's perspectives are important and valuable.

GROOMER Feedback Protocol

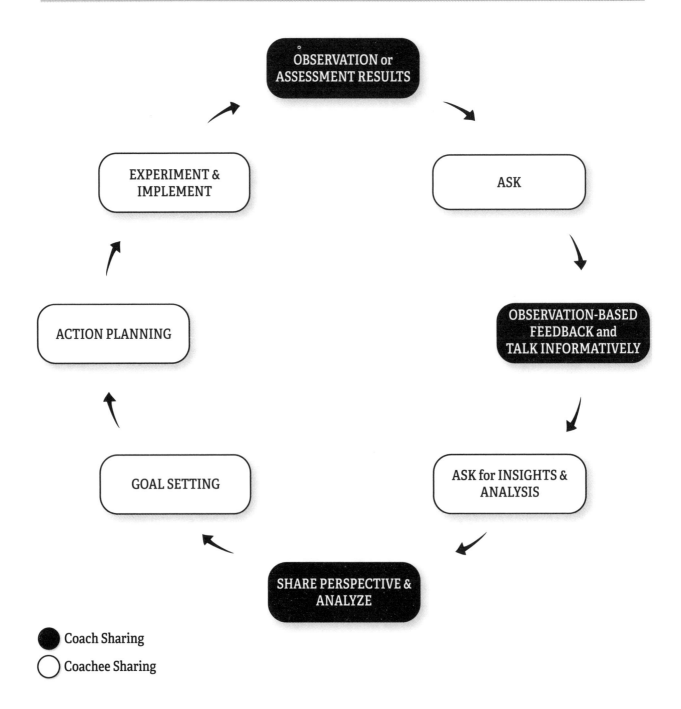

Coach Sharing
Coachee Sharing

1. Observe or Discuss Assessment Results

2. Ask
   Ask coachees for their perspective of how they thought the observed session went or how they would summarize or analyze the assessment results.

3. Observation-Based Feedback and Talk Informatively
   Offer observational feedback or provide simple assessment results, not an interpretation or why you think it's important—just data. Give specific and concrete examples of what you witnessed; use

speaking, nonverbal cues, body language, and objective, descriptive, narrative, and sensory language about actions. For example, say, "When you gave instructions to the children to get ready to go outdoors, you said, 'Put your coats on.' You did not tell them what to do after their coats were on." Don't say, "You're very unclear when you give children directions."

4. Ask for Insights and Analysis

Ask coachees how this information is meaningful and has value, and what impact the information has for them. Ask if they can see any goals or actions they might consider; avoid telling them what you think their goal should be.

5. Share Perspective and Analyze

If necessary, share your perspective of the information—the meaning, relevance, and importance you perceive. If not necessary, validate the coachee's analysis.

6. Goal Setting

Given the data, ask coachees to identify any goals they want to achieve. Follow their lead, and if appropriate, offer additional or extended suggestions. Be mindful not to overwhelm coachees with too many goals at one time.

7. Action Planning

Ask coachees to brainstorm options for actions they could take to achieve each goal. Offer additional suggestions if needed. Establish a time frame for accomplishing each action.

8. Experiment and Implement

As coachees start to implement actions, either continue to make observations and start the feedback cycle again, or have reflective conversations to discern their progress.

Giving feedback is a way to bridge the intent-impact gap. Here are some steps to follow:

- Inquire regarding the coachee's intent.
- Provide observation.
- Describe what resulted from the person's action, what the impact was.

For example, you could say, "You have interrupted your colleague four times in your conversation. I notice she has stopped talking and trying to share her ideas." Or, "When you gave instructions to the children to get ready to go outdoors, you said, 'Put your coats on.' You did not tell them what to do next—for instance, to then line up at the door or to go to the carpet. I then noticed three children were running around the room. You then put one child in time-out for running, and he wasn't allowed to go outdoors. It may be worth considering how the child's behavior may have been related to the lack of clear instructions for what to do once the children had their coats on. How might this inform your decision about how to avoid those behaviors and the need to discipline him?"

"We must remember the simple truth: the human soul does not want to be fixed, it wants simply to be seen and heard."
—Parker J. Palmer

Giving Feedback Formula Worksheet

Giving Professional Feedback

1. "When you . . ." (Note the behavior; describe it as specifically as possible.)

_____

2. "I noticed . . ." (Tell what you observed regarding how the coachee's behavior affected a person/child or the impact it had on the environment/situation. Briefly provide this information so they can consider the meaning, implication, or relevance for themselves.)

_____

_____

3. "Is that relevant or helpful for you?" (Ask if and how that information matters from their perspective.)

_____

_____

From Feedback to Action

4. "I wonder if you might want to consider or explore . . ." (If necessary, share why you think it might be relevant to further consider or reframe this in a larger context.)

_____

_____

5. "Because . . ." (Why you believe this would be beneficial.)

_____

_____

6. "What do you think?" (Invite and hear the response; explore options.)

_____

_____

Giving Feedback Formula Worksheet

Giving Personal Feedback

1. "When you . . ." (Note the behavior; describe it as specifically as possible.)

_____

2. "I felt . . ." (Tell how the behavior affects you in just one or two words—frustrated, angry, pleased, and so on.)

_____

_____

_____

3. "Because I . . ." (Share why you are affected in that way.)

_____

_____

_____

From Feedback to Negotiation in a Relationship

4. "I would like . . ." (What you would like the person to consider doing.)

_____

_____

5. "Because . . ." (Why you believe it will help.)

_____

_____

6. "What do you think?" (Invite and hear the response; explore options.)

_____

_____

_____

Coaching Tools

These tools are nondirective, or a lighter scaffolding approach on the continuum.

TALKING INFORMATIVELY, OR NARRATION

Coaches need to examine and be mindful of the language they use and how they speak with coachees. My colleague Tom Drummond developed a college curriculum, *Connecting to Children*, that includes a module to help early childhood educators examine types of interactive language adults use when speaking with children (Drummond 2002). The types of language can be classified into two groups—demanding or nondemanding language (see table on page 122). These types of interactive language are also applicable to and useful for coaches when speaking with adults. Demanding language carries a level of power and authority from the speaker that is not necessarily needed or useful. This is particularly true if you want coachees to take the initiative for their own learning and to become more self-aware. All demanding language expects a response or an answer. Demanding language does not fully empower the other person to take initiative; instead the person is following the speaker's lead. Clearly when you give a direction or make a suggestion, it leaves the person with only two options: to comply with the instruction or suggestion, or not to comply, either overtly or passively, and not do what they were instructed. Questions are a type of demanding language. Even open-ended questions are a form of expectation or continuation of the conversation. This doesn't make questions bad—it is just important to be aware that they carry a level of power with them, a demand for a response, and there are times this may not be desired or needed.

The value of using nondemanding language is that you can lead by informing rather than telling or directing. It allows the information and data you communicate to affect the coachee, giving them time to think, analyze, and respond or decide what to do. Talking informatively is a non-demanding type of communication. Talking informatively with children is a way to give a cue, offering them the opportunity to decide what to do with the information. This promotes initiative and allows children to take the lead in their own learning process. The same is true when communicating with adults. By talking informatively, coaches can provide information in a neutral way, which can offer a cue or expand people's awareness and perspective, inform their thinking about their actions, and allow them to decide what to do with the information. It is an empowering way of communicating and interacting that transfers power and, ultimately, the responsibility for their own learning, to coachees. While waiting to see what the coachee does with the information, it's important for coaches to remain quiet without immediately following up with a question. This can be difficult and a hard habit to break. Pause and witness how the information affects the coachee. Does it make them ask questions, do they seem to gain insight into the situation, or do they have too little awareness or knowledge to know what to do with the information? The coachee's response will inform the coach about what actions to take and from which end of the continuum to choose a facilitation strategy to support the coachee.

Coaches are very practiced in asking questions but not so experienced in talking informatively. Watch a video of an observation of either a child or an adult, and practice talking informatively by writing down the language you would use to share your observations with the learner in that situation without teaching or directing. Or watch a colleague do something (anything) and practice speaking informatively after observing them. It takes practice to know what to highlight or focus on that could offer the person some perspective or insight. Keep it simple. This takes practice.

How could you use talking informatively as a way to support a coachee? How could you increase your usage of this tool by 50 percent? What would that require of you?

Pause & Reflect

_____

_____

_____

_____

_____

Types of Interactive Language

Type	Demanding		
	Direction	**Tutorial**	**Query**
Definition	Statements that tell someone what or how to do something or that instruct them on a topic. Statements that require or directly command an action that the person must do or not do.	Leading questions used for review, reminders, or teaching. They are not open-ended questions. These questions have an implied agenda or point to make. The person asking the question already knows the answer.	Following questions asked from authentic inquiry, curiosity, and wonder. They are open-ended questions. The person asking the question does not know the answer.
Example	With children: "Throw your cup and snack away." With adults: "You need to change your negative attitude," or "At circle time, encourage children to ask more questions."	With children: "What do you need to do to stay warm when you go outside?" With adults: "What do you know you need to do when you have a negative attitude?" or "Do you think allowing the children to ask more questions or be more actively engaged at circle time might help the situation?"	With children: "What are all the ways we could stay warm outside?" With adults: "Are you aware you're speaking negatively?" or "What happened when you let the children ask questions at circle time?"

(Drummond 2002)

Nondemanding

Type	Informative	Social
Definition	Statements that use descriptive sensory language to describe actions, speech, and verbal and nonverbal cues. Tell the coachee what you see and hear, not what you think something meant or why it was important. These statements are facts and observations given to describe, inform, and enlighten.	Statements given for social reasons. This category includes repeating what someone just said and anything that does not fit into the other categories.
Example	With children: "You don't have a coat on and we are going outside." With adults: "You just said, 'It's impossible to do that' three times in the last five minutes," or "I noticed the children got very animated and had a lot of ideas as they started to ask more questions at circle time. Over half the children were talking and engaged."	Phrases like *okay*, *hello*, *oh really*, *I don't know*, *could be*, *fine*, and *that's good*.

BRIDGING THE INTENT-IMPACT GAP REFLECTION

Again, an intent-impact gap is when someone tries to help a situation in one way, but their behavior ends up having a very different effect than what was intended, and the person is unaware of the gap. This can happen between adults and children, children and children, and adults and adults. Coaches can help a person become aware of this gap. In this situation, the most efficient coaching tools are to ask questions and to give feedback by talking informatively.

- If the person's behavior seemed intentional, ask about the intent. For example,
  - "What was your intention when you gave instructions to the children to get ready to go outside?"

- If you think the person is unaware of the behavior, ask if they realize what they just did. Provide observational feedback using "Talking Informatively" to provide information to describe what happened. For example,
  - "Are you aware that you have interrupted your colleague four times in your conversation?"
  - "When you gave instructions to the children to get ready to go outdoors, you said, 'Put your coats on.' You did not tell them what to do next once their coats were on."

- In addition, describe the result of the person's action—the impact— again using narrative description or talking informatively. For example,
  - "I notice your colleague has stopped talking and is no longer trying to share her ideas."
  - "After the children had their coats on, three children were running around the room. You then put one child in time-out for running, and he wasn't allowed to go outdoors."

- Ask if this was the intended outcome or how this narrative information might be useful. Does knowing the impact make the coachee want to think about or change their behavior or how they might approach a similar situation in the future? Give them time to receive the information, analyze it, and think. Thinking takes time. See what they do with the awareness and the information before talking more, asking a question, or adding your own perspectives. If they don't seem to make a connection between their behavior and the result, offer your thoughts or ask additional questions to help them gain some perspective and deepen their reflection. For example,

- o "How does it affect you knowing that your colleague has stopped talking and is no longer trying to share her ideas?"
- o "What value would it be to ask her what happened from her perspective?"

● Finally, help the person consider different ways to change the behavior to get the desired results. For example,

- o "If you are not aware when you are interrupting, what are some options or strategies that might help you become more aware of this behavior?"
- o "What do you want to do in the future to ensure that you and your colleague are both able to share ideas?"

Here's another example of when someone's intention for their behavior or action did not have the desired impact, and what coaching strategies I used to close the intent-impact gap. I was coaching a teacher, Sue, who wanted to communicate better with her coteacher about their weekly lesson plans. Sue felt like most of this responsibility had fallen on her, which she did not like. She had not shared her concern with her colleague. Sue's goal was to increase her communication skills, and her action plan included being very clear and less vague about what her coteacher needed to do. After developing this plan, Sue told her colleague exactly what she wanted her to do, and in an effort to be very clear, she gave directive instructions. But when she did this, not only did her colleague not do the tasks Sue told her to do, her colleague also got upset with her. Sue was a little surprised and confused by her reaction. Sue's plan of being clear by being directive was intended to increase communication and, ultimately, to share the workload. But her behavior produced the opposite effect. Through coaching, Sue realized that her directive delivery of telling her colleague what to do may be what didn't work. Sue became aware that her approach with her colleague was not respectful of her coteacher's ideas or of their equal partnership. She realized she might have come across as being bossy; this helped her understand her colleague's reaction. Sue decided to start a conversation with her colleague about her concern over how they were collaborating on lesson plans, and then ask her how she would like to approach this situation. This did end up being a more successful strategy.

Coaches can use the Bridging the Intent-Impact Gap Reflection to help coachees identify any gaps between what they intended and the actual result. This activity is often used during the Experiment component of the cycle of change in the GROOMER Framework. This approach is also beneficial during the Options component to help people brainstorm ways to change their actions.

GOALS AND ACTION PLANNING

Chapter 3 includes a description of how to use the SMART Goals approach to goal setting. Coaches can use the SMART Goal Worksheet to guide coachees in ensuring their goal is a SMART goal. This form can be downloaded at www.redleafpress.org/transformationalcoaching. Chapter 8 describes several other types of goal- and action-planning forms that can be helpful to clarify and document goals with a coachee. (These forms are also available at www.redleafpress.org/transformationalcoaching.)

Slide along the Continuum When Selecting Targeted Facilitation Tools

These targeted facilitation tools are designed to provide as much or as little structured and directive support as the coachee needs. Accordingly, some of these tools aligned with consulting will be more directive, active, and leading with coachees, providing more structured support. When using such tools, the coachee will be more passive, following the coach's lead and taking less initiative. When using facilitation tools aligned with coaching strategies, a coach will provide lighter scaffolding or a less directive approach that is more open-ended, shifting the power of action, initiative, and leadership to the coachee. Using the tools aligned with coaching will foster more self-awareness, critical thinking, and capacity building in the coachee. We want coachees to learn and use these targeted tools for themselves when they encounter new challenges in the future. The intention is for coachees to become more independent, improve their practices, and sustain change themselves over time. It is important to assess how much support is actually needed, wanted, and tolerated to achieve the desired outcomes.

Reflection in Action

Take time to reflect on what you learned in this chapter and its impact on and value for you.

_____

_____

_____

_____

Key messages:

- Intentionally choose either structured and more directive targeted tools or more reflective and nondirective targeted tools to facilitate the coachee's learning and change process, based on individual needs.
- Consulting facilitation tools are modeling and feedback.
- Coaching facilitation tools are talking informatively, intent/impact gap reflection, and goals/action planning.

Objective: What are key words or phrases, quotes, concepts, stories, activities, or ideas that stand out or stick for you personally?

_____

_____

Reflective: What part of this feels affirming or inspiring? What aspect feels like a stretch or might be challenging for you?

_____

_____

_____

Interpretive: What was most relevant and meaningful for you? How does this information affect your work or coaching practices?

_____

_____

_____

Decisional: What implications does this have for your actions in the future? What are you most committed to putting into action?

_____

_____

Tools for Busting Obstacles and Barriers

The GROOMER Framework for Change model has seven components that guide coaches in their work to help coachees focus and reflect on their behaviors in order to take intentional action for sustainable change. This chapter examines the Obstacles and Barriers component of the change model; these are common problems people face when trying to close the gap between where they are and where they want to be. Most people, both coaches and coachees, will face at least one challenge related to limitations in the following areas: Awareness, Attitudes, Motivation, Emotions, Stress, and Skills (AAMESS). This component is one of the unique and most pivotal aspects of the GROOMER Framework for Change. It is important for coaches to be able to identify and have strategies for overcoming predictable obstacles and challenges that most people face when trying to improve or change their practices and habits. These AAMESS barriers are often where coaches are stumped or challenged themselves when helping coachees master new skills, adopt new professional practices, and overcome motivation or attitude challenges, or when helping people deal with stress that blocks their ability to perform basic tasks and meet professional demands. This chapter includes several additional targeted tools for busting through each of the AAMESS obstacles and barriers. The suggested targeted facilitation tools enable coaches to help a person address, overcome, or transform each obstacle. These targeted tools or activities can be incorporated into your own or your coachee's Targeted Action Plan. This chapter also includes suggestions, activity instructions, and/or worksheets coaches can use to help learners overcome common obstacles and barriers (forms are available at www.redleafpress.org/transformationalcoaching). Remember to practice and complete these activities yourself, addressing barriers you are facing in any area of your life, particularly those related to expanding your coaching and facilitation strategies and skills. You will be better prepared to facilitate coachees using these tools if you have personally implemented them for your own growth and learning.

Targeted Tools to Bust Obstacles and Barriers

Awareness	Attitude	Motivation	Emotions	Stress	Skills
Talk informatively	Reframe disempowering perspectives and negative thinking	Clarify alignment with goals and expectations	Increase self-regulation	Increase response-ability	Practice and repeat simple habits
Give feedback	Shift negative attitudes and self-talk	Examine cost/payoff	Strengthen protective factors using DARS	Expand ability to respond to demands	Use skill/will matrix
Reflect on intent-impact gap	Create mental billboards		Practice trigger teaching and activity	Decrease demands	Use five guidelines to deal with homeostasis
Use E + R = O to increase response-ability			Strengthen leadership resilience using DERLS	Start where you have a choice	
				Do stress reflection activity	
				Empty out using REmember list	
				Expand domains of self-responsibility	
				Be proactive, not reactive	

Busting Awareness Barriers

Chapter 2 discussed how to cultivate essential qualities for change, especially the quality of reflection. Reflection is also the primary tool for busting any barrier related to awareness. Awareness is a barrier in multiple ways.

When people lack self-awareness, they are not very aware of their own thoughts, feelings, and motivations. When people lack interpersonal awareness, they have limited awareness of their interpersonal dynamics with and impact on other people. When individuals lack a general level of consciousness, they don't see what's going on around them or notice any details. Awareness is 80 percent of the game when it comes to change—either recognizing that change is needed or identifying what needs to change. You can't change what you can't see. Busting the awareness barrier, then, means bringing those things into focus so a person can identify how best to move forward. We've already discussed several awareness-expanding tools in this book, but I will summarize them here.

FEEDBACK

Feedback is a tool to help people gain more awareness and to make informed choices. In chapter 6, Guidelines for Giving feedback and the GROOMER Feedback Protocol were introduced.

TALKING INFORMATIVELY

Talking informatively is another tool for expanding awareness. In chapter 6, a detailed description of how to talk informatively is provided. Speaking narratively provides information in a way that helps people see things they might not have been able to see on their own. When you provide only information without any commentary, the coachee gains a greater awareness and understanding about what's happening. What's more, the coachee is free to use that information to inform decisions, actions, or ways to reframe their perspective or thoughts. Talking informatively also helps the coach gain insight on how to individualize for the coachee by observing what they do or don't do with the information provided. Again, this is a less directive coaching tool that helps transfer more power to the coachee.

INTENT-IMPACT GAP REFLECTION TOOL

Chapter 6 also introduced the Intent-Impact Gap Reflection tool, which is an excellent tool to use when coachees are not aware that their behavior had a negative impact on another person or a different result than they were expecting. This tool helps them reflect on their behavior, consider their intent, and gain perspective on the actual effect of their behavior.

This new knowledge enables people to make choices about how to increase their awareness when they are behaving in that way and then modify their behavior or put action plans in place to change their behaviors to achieve their desired impact.

INCREASE RESPONSIBILITY (E + R = O)

In his book *The Success Principles*, Jack Canfield (2015, 4) says, "Taking 100% responsibility means you acknowledge that you create everything that happens to you. It means you understand that *you* are the cause of all of your experiences." He shares a simple formula that illustrates this idea of being 100 percent responsible for your life if you want to create a life you want. The formula is E + R = O (Event + Response = Outcome). He explains it like this:

> The idea is that every outcome you experience . . . is the result of how you have responded to an earlier event or events in your life. If you don't like the outcomes you are currently getting, there are two basic choices you can make. 1) You can blame the event (E) for your lack of results (O). . . . 2) You can instead simply change your responses (R) to the events (E)—the way things are—until you get the outcomes (O) you want. . . . If you don't like your outcomes, change your responses. (6–7)

This is a powerful formula that not only had a big impact on my own life but helped me better coach people who were not taking much responsibility for their own actions. I eventually created the following E + R = O worksheets (pages 135–36) to help them reflect and then document how their thinking was at work in their lives, especially as it related to them not experiencing the outcomes they wanted. This activity and facilitation guideline describes how to support coachees to rethink their responses to get the desired outcomes. This activity not only examines the Obstacle but also incorporates other GROOMER model components, such as Reality, Options, and Goals.

When coachees complain about specific situations or don't like their current outcomes, use this formula to guide them to reflect about what the current situation is, what happened, how they responded, and what the resulting outcome was. The important thing is to help them focus on where they have control (which is in their response), not on the situation or other people, which is where most people tend to focus their complaints.

Review the Current Reality

- Discuss the coachee's situation and identify the current outcome they are not happy with or don't like. In part 1 of the worksheet, write that outcome in the right-side box labeled "Undesirable Outcome." This outcome is essentially a Goal in the GROOMER Framework for Change model.

- Sometimes the coachee is clear on what the event is, and sometimes they need help unraveling it. An event can be a situation (like a new center arrival/departure protocol); it can be something someone says or doesn't say, or does or doesn't do (like a child hitting another child); or it can be an act of God (like a snowstorm). Record the description of the event in the left-side box labeled "Challenging Event."

- Then discuss how the coachee responded to the event. Explore their thoughts, feelings, and actions—including verbal and nonverbal actions—and record them in the center box labeled "Your Responses." Frequently, the responsive behaviors that get coachees in trouble are nonverbal, like eye rolling, crossing their arms and leaning back in a conversation, or not getting down at a child's eye level.

Create Options for Future/Potential Actions
The second area to examine is what the coachee wants or wishes could happen given the very same event or situation.

- To help shift the coachee's responses to create better outcomes, begin by copying the event to the "Same Challenging Event" box in part 2 of the worksheet. In other words, the original event needs to stay the same—this is the one thing that doesn't change in the revised version of the formula, since the triggering situation is not typically in the person's control and could happen again.

- Next, clarify what outcome they *do* want when the same challenging event occurs. They have to decide given any situation—good or bad—what they want to experience. Record this in the "Desirable Outcome" box on the right side. Be sure to do this *before* examining their alternative responses.

- Last, identify how the coachee will need and want to respond to that same event so the outcome they hope for could occur. Again, help them consider what thoughts they might need to shift or reframe, what emotional reactions they might need to change, or what they could do or say differently. And don't forget to talk about those nonverbal actions! Record these in the "Alternative Responses" box in the middle. This is a brainstorming activity that would be part of the Options component in the GROOMER model.

> *"Life is 10% of what happens to me and 90% how I react to it."*
> *—Charles Swindoll*

Once the coachee has clarified some options for the Response (R) box in part 2 of the worksheet, they need to do some planning. Just going through this process is very eye-opening. Awareness is the first step to change, but it will also take action and commitment to implement different ways of behaving, and it can take some time for the new actions to become habits that stick. While the coachee is implementing their chosen actions, they are in the Experiment component of the GROOMER Framework. During this time, they are likely to need encouragement, continued reflection, and help analyzing what's working and what's not. They may need to Refine or modify their strategies to eventually create the outcomes they want.

You'll find a completed sample *E + R = O* worksheet and a blank worksheet with simple instructions on pages 135–36 and the online appendix at www.redleafpress.org/transformationalcoaching.

Busting Attitude Barriers

Limiting or negative attitudes are a common barrier for most of us at some point. Negative self-talk is one of the most prevalent limiting attitudes in the people I have worked with that gets in the way of them closing the gap between where they are right now and where they want to be. The following tools are designed to help coaches facilitate reflection and exploration about attitudes, beliefs, and perspectives. The goal is to help people shift or reframe any limiting or negative attitudes and adopt more empowering attitudes.

> *"Remember—80% of success is mindset, attitudes and beliefs. 20% is implementation. Consequently, having the tools to change what is going on in your head can have immense positive impact on your life and in your work. Today's thoughts, attitudes and beliefs create tomorrow's outcomes."*
> *—Jonathan Manske*

REFRAME DISEMPOWERING PERSPECTIVES AND NEGATIVE THINKING

Perspective is a point of view or way of looking at a particular set of events. Perspectives

E + R = O Worksheet, *Sample*

Instructions—Part 1

1. Choose an Event (other person, circumstance) you find challenging.
2. Write the current undesirable Outcome (results, experience) you usually have regarding this event.
3. List your current Response (thought, feeling, or action) to this event that is producing the current outcome. What do you think, feel, or do when this event happens?

Current		
Challenging Event	**Your Responses**	**Undesirable Outcome**
E	**+** **R**	**=** **O**
A colleague interrupts me all the time.	I tell her she's rude and to please stop! I shake my head and say, "You're doing it again!" several times during a meeting. I'm frustrated and irritated.	I don't like working with her anymore. She's defensive.

Instructions—Part 2

4. Identify what desirable Outcome you would like to have or experience regarding the *exact same* Event you find challenging. Copy the same words from the current challenging Event column in part 1.
5. Identify at least one perception, belief, attitude, thought, feeling, or action you can change to be able to Respond more positively and effectively to this Event to get the desirable outcome you want. (Ideally, identify three possible alternative responses.)

Future/Potential		
Same Challenging Event	**Alternative Responses**	**Desirable Outcome**
E	**+** **R**	**=** **O**
A colleague interrupts me all the time.	Take a breath before speaking. Use an "I statement" and let her know how I feel when she interrupts me and the impact it has on me. Share about me, not her. Ask if she is aware she's doing this. Discuss with her what would be a helpful and respectful way for me to let her know when she's interrupting.	I want to be calm. I want to like working with her. I want her to be more open to my feedback.

E + R = O Worksheet

Instructions—Part 1

1. Choose an Event (other person, circumstance) you find challenging.
2. Write the current undesirable Outcome (results, experience) you usually have regarding this event.
3. List your current Response (thought, feeling, or action) to this event that is producing the current outcome. What do you think, feel, or do when this event happens?

Current		
Challenging Event	Your Responses	Undesirable Outcome
E +	R =	O

Instructions—Part 2

4. Identify what desirable Outcome you would like to have or experience regarding the *exact same* Event you find challenging. Copy the same words from the current challenging Event column in part 1.
5. Identify at least one perception, belief, attitude, thought, feeling, or action you can change to be able to Respond more positively and effectively to this Event to get the desirable outcome you want. (Ideally, identify three possible alternative responses.)

Future/Potential		
Same Challenging Event	Alternative Responses	Desirable Outcome
E +	R =	O

are based on beliefs — they come from your frame of reference. When people believe that their negative thoughts, perspectives, or beliefs are truth, they often create mind-sets or attitudes that are limiting, negative, and disempowering. Your perspective, not your circumstances, determines your experiences in life. The good news is you can choose to change your perspective at any time. The first step in changing disempowering perspectives is to identify your negative perspectives. Once you've done that, making a change in perspective is like changing any other habit. It takes intention, motivation, time, and practice. You can increase self-regulation and gain control of your responses to your life and your circumstances by intentionally choosing a perspective that will positively influence your choices. Following is an activity to help you recognize common disempowering perspectives that may be affecting your day-to-day life and how to choose and identify where to start in changing and reframing perspectives in ways that will positively affect your life and improve your effectiveness as a coach. You can share this same reflection activity with your coachees as a foundational assessment or when it becomes apparent that a specific limiting attitude is in the way, needs to be reframed, and necessitates an action plan.

DISEMPOWERING PERSPECTIVES ACTIVITY

Check the boxes next to the perspectives you commonly experience. Star the boxes next to the two most influential perspectives you would like to change and reframe.

Fifteen Disempowering Perspectives

☐ **Negative filter:** You focus only on the negative in a situation and ignore the good. By doing so, the negative seems larger or worse than it really is.

☐ **Black-and-white thinking:** You view everything in extremes — all good or bad. Nothing is in the gray zone.

☐ **Universalization:** Your thinking is characterized by "always" and "never" and is often based on limited or unverified information. You make conclusions or false interpretations based on a single situation or a limited piece of evidence. If something bad happens once, you predict it will happen over and over again.

☐ **Assumptions:** You come to conclusions about another person's actions or intentions without any real evidence. This is sometimes called *mind reading*, as if you can somehow "just know" what another person is thinking or feeling.

☐ **Catastrophizing:** You expect disaster to strike in your life. A common symptom is "what if?" thinking, and an underlying catalyst is a lack of trust in yourself and your capacity to adapt to change.

☐ **Personalization:** This is a tendency to assume that everything happening around you is somehow about you. This often results in disappointments and emotional responses such as hurt feelings or anger.

☐ **Shoulds:** With this thinking, you believe that you and others in your life need to follow a list of rules you have created. This tendency is tied to judging and finding fault in yourself and others.

☐ **Labeling:** This generalized way of thinking characterizes or stereotypes yourself or other people based on limited information or even a single experience or quality. It fails to recognize that people are complex and have multiple dimensions. This can lead to prejudice and bias toward others.

☐ **Blaming:** This is a way of thinking that makes other people responsible for your problems or your discomfort.

☐ **Victim thinking:** You feel as if you lack any power, control, or choice over what happens to or around you and whether or not you are happy or effective in life.

☐ **Being right:** This thinking centers on the need to always be right or correct, and to prove this to others. This does not allow for considering other points of view and often causes distance in relationships.

☐ **Not being wrong:** This way of thinking is fear based and centers on the need to prove one's worth by proving you are correct, defending your opinion, or avoiding getting in trouble for being wrong.

☐ **Fear of failure:** This attitude views mistakes and failure as a threat or hazard that should be avoided at all costs rather than as a learning opportunity. This often closes one off to other ways of thinking and doesn't allow for flexibility in thinking.

☐ **Emotional reasoning:** You believe that any thought you have must be true, including feelings or perceptions about yourself based on distorted or false thoughts or beliefs.

☐ **Fallacy of change:** This is about assuming you can convince or cajole other people and expect them to change to suit you. With this way of thinking, your happiness depends on others changing, and it places your happiness in another person's hands rather than in your own.

(McKay, Davis, and Fanning 2007; Elmore 2011)

REFRAMING FEAR OF FAILURE AND MAKING MISTAKES

The perspective "fear of failure" combined with "not being wrong" come up quite frequently in coaching, usually when people start experiencing anxiety, concern, or resistance to change because they are afraid to make mistakes. To help, coaches can inquire about what early messages the coachee received about making mistakes, either negative or positive. For example, "If you can't do it right, don't do anything at all" or "If you don't succeed, keep trying!" Both experiences become part of a person's frame of reference and can affect them powerfully, often in unconscious ways. Document this conversation on the following worksheet when you are together or give it to the coachee to complete and bring back to discuss at a later time.

MESSAGES ABOUT MISTAKES ACTIVITY

In the left column, write any *positive* messages you have received in your life about mistakes, failures, and constraints. In the center column, write *negative* messages you have received about mistakes, failures, and constraints. In the right column, *reframe the negative messages* into more positive messages.

Positive Messages	Negative Messages	Reframed Message
_____	_____	_____
_____	_____	_____
_____	_____	_____
_____	_____	_____
_____	_____	_____
_____	_____	_____
_____	_____	_____

USING MENTAL BILLBOARDS TO CHANGE UNWANTED THOUGHTS OR HABITS

Mental imagery is a powerful way to shift perspectives, learn new skills, or change undesirable habits. Creating a mental billboard—a simple visual cue or word(s)—is one way to help focus attention on or move toward a new way of thinking or acting. Focusing on what you want is critical because your energy follows what you focus on. The principle is this: focus on what you want, not what you worry about, because what you focus on expands.

You or your coachee can do this by mentally visualizing on an internal billboard, or you can create a visual sign to post in a location where you will see it frequently. However you want to approach this, the idea is to see and refer to this message frequently while you are in the process of adopting the new habit or thought pattern.

- Identify one word, reminder, or quote to help you focus on what you want.

- Make a sign that will remind you of the positive action or behavior you want to take.

- I created a small sign book called *Creating Ease in a Day's Work Sign Book*, with many helpful messages you can put on your desk or nightstand (Hine 2011). These messages are focused on transforming stress by reframing limiting thoughts or adopting habits that reduce overwhelm and create calm. There are examples of these signs on the following worksheet.

Try out the following activity yourself and have your coachees use it as well.

□ □

MENTAL BILLBOARDS

Use this activity to change unwanted thoughts and habits.

- Identify the habit/behavior you want to change (for example, to stop giving advice or to pause and listen more):

_____

- Close your eyes and make a very big, bright, colorful picture in your mind—a mental image—of what you see just before the unwanted habit/behavior begins (like seeing and feeling yourself getting excited, agitated, or upset about what someone is saying). The more unpleasant or dissatisfying this picture, the better. Then use a mental eraser to clear away the picture.

- Next make a big, bright, colorful picture of the way you would like to be (your desired state)—the sort of person who would respond differently, with more choices. Make the picture of this "new you" as positive as you can. (For example, you feel very calm and patient and interested in what the other person is saying.)

- Now make a large mental image of a billboard with one or two words that will remind you of the action you want to take to be successful in achieving your goal. Imagine this billboard in bright colors, with flashing lights and large, simple words (example: "calm and listen").

Whenever you find yourself on the verge of going back to this unwanted behavior, imagine the new, positive mental image of the way you would like to feel and the large, bright billboard reminding you of the behavior you want to exhibit.

Write a few ideas of what you could put on a mental billboard:

_____

_____

_____

Make your mental billboard into a sign and post where it will help you remember to practice the actions and behaviors you want to develop.

Busting Motivation Barriers

Change requires motivation from either external demands or an intrinsic force. When goals are externally imposed, it's very common to have difficulty implementing the actions or plans needed to achieve the goals. The obstacles here are likely issues related to motivation. These will need to be explored and clarified. Exposing the reality of coachees' lack of motivation is important, and coaches need to facilitate this without adding any pressure, judgment, or blame. It's important to remain neutral so coachees can examine and voice their concerns honestly. Sometimes early childhood providers simply don't understand the reasons they should make an expected change in behaviors or actions. If so, they may need either information or help to bridge the gap between a given expectation or goal and how it is related to what is meaningful or valuable to the coachee or beneficial to the children in their care. Some educators have strong personal values and beliefs that are at odds with certain expected professional practices, licensing requirements, or quality performance indicators. Topics that elicit strong reactions often center on fundamental care procedures on eating routines, diapering or toileting procedures, approaches to discipline, and how to handle specific challenging, and often-triggering, behaviors of children, such as spitting, swearing, aggression, or whining. Many times these conflicting values are culture based, and an open discussion will be needed to determine how to resolve this conflict. Until you identify and discuss a reason for the coachee's lack of or conflicting motivation, the coachee's change plan won't work or won't last; they will eventually revert to old, preferred practices. For change to occur, it's critical to deal with such issues of motivation. The transformational coaching approach is focused on exactly this—exploring the underlying reasons, values, or beliefs that might be in the way of making necessary changes. Through open dialogue, inquiry, and authentic curiosity, coaches can facilitate meaningful ways for coachees to reframe any limiting perceptions, find solutions, or make modifications to be successful.

CLARIFYING MOTIVATIONAL ALIGNMENT WITH EXPECTATIONS AND GOALS

Even when their goal is intrinsically motivated, people can also encounter obstacles to achieving their desired results. It is not uncommon for people to start implementing their plans and then realize their plan is more complex than anticipated. This may cause some hesitancy or inner conflict that will need to be identified or clarified. Or it might just require a thoughtful, detailed conversation about creating additional targeted action plans to address each new detail or consequence of the original plan.

Note: I recommend using the Six Stages of Change Readiness Assessment to gauge the readiness and willingness a person may have for making changes in any specific area, as this affects their motivation. (See chapter 1.)

Motivation is often at play in areas in which people are less open to change. To stimulate efficient self-change, coaches need to use effective coaching strategies that match a person's motivation readiness. The early stages of change rely primarily on raising consciousness, self-reflection, and self-evaluation while moving into action. But insight alone does not bring about behavior change. It will also take overt actions, with strategic plans for modifying behaviors, thoughts, and feelings.

EXAMINING COSTS AND PAYOFFS

Use the Cost/Payoff strategy when someone persists in using a negative or limiting behavior. People cannot change what they can't see. This examination can help identify what is motivating their behavior and reveal why the person keeps repeating it. It increases the coachee's awareness of both the payoff and the costs of the behavior.

Facilitation Guidelines

Start the inquiry with the payoffs. Ask the person the types of questions listed on the next page to identify why they keep repeating the negative or limiting behavior. The reason they keep using that behavior is because they actually get a "payoff" from the negative behavior—although the payoff is usually unconscious and they have never examined it. After they have a clear understanding of the payoffs, ask them about the "cost" using the following types of questions to identify the possible costs or disadvantages to continuing the challenging behavior. This may be a long list, or it might only be one really big and critically important cost. All it takes is something on the cost side that outweighs all the payoffs to create a shift in motivation to make behavioral change.

People will not change their behavior until they see that the cost outweighs the payoff. If they choose not to change their behavior, don't despair. By reflecting, they have actually changed their consciousness, and that can never go backward. They can't unknow what they just became aware of. I have had coachees who choose not to change the behavior because the payoff is too great. Be patient. With time things might change, but it needs to be their choice! When the coachee engages in the challenging behavior, they will now have a level of self-awareness that previously wasn't there, which often adds weight to the cost side of the equation. Remember, we can't force people to change, but we can continue to dialogue about their increasing awareness over time and assess their level of readiness to change the behavior. Review the lists on the next page for effective ways to ask your coachee about the payoffs and costs of a negative behavior, which can be anything—avoiding conflict, not completing work, being late, arguing with teammates, gossiping, using ineffective professional practices, or reverting to bad habits.

IDENTIFYING PAYOFFS AND COSTS ACTIVITY— PART 1

You get something from this negative or limiting behavior, or you wouldn't do it. Let's explore what this could be.

Payoff	Cost
What benefit do you get from this behavior, even though you know it's not a great behavior?	Why do you think this behavior is a problem or limiting you?
What are the positive outcomes of behaving this way?	What are the negative outcomes when you do this?
What do you get to avoid or not do by engaging in this behavior?	What price do you pay when you do this? What price do others around you pay when you do this?
What positive results do you experience as a result of this behavior, even if the behavior is undesirable, limiting, or negative?	How does this inhibit, delay, or compromise your success?
What's one reason you chose to behave this way the last time you did it?	How do you feel when you act this way?
What are your beliefs or thoughts about this behavior that might be a payoff or benefit to you?	What are your beliefs or thoughts about this behavior that might be a cost or disadvantage to you?
Make a list of all the different reasons for continuing this behavior; there could be many.	Make a list of all the different ways this behavior is costly; there might be just one big thing or many.

□ □

IDENTIFYING PAYOFFS AND COSTS ACTIVITY— PART 2

Instructions: Identify a challenging, negative, or limiting behavior that you continue to do even though you know it's not in your best interest. Start with the payoffs. List the benefits—what you get out of this behavior and why you continue to do it. When the payoffs are clear, move on to the costs. List what negative outcomes or results you experience from this behavior. Note: You will likely not change your behavior until the costs outweigh the payoffs.

Payoff	**Cost**
_____	_____
_____	_____
_____	_____
_____	_____
_____	_____
_____	_____
_____	_____
_____	_____

□ □

Busting Emotion Barriers

Emotions can become barriers to making changes. Some of the common emotional challenges people encounter when trying to reach goals and change their professional practices is a limitation or lack of emotional self-regulation. According to the Center on the Developing Child at Harvard University (2017), "Self-regulation helps us to draw upon the right skills at the right time, manage our responses to the world, and resist inappropriate responses. In the brain, self-regulation includes both *intentional* and *automatic* processes. The proper balance ensures appropriately responsive and productive actions.

- **Automatic self-regulation** is our rapid, impulse-directed response (also called the 'fight or flight' response) that is needed for urgent or threatening situations.

- **Intentional self-regulation** is our conscious, planful, and proactive response needed for achieving goals."

When coaching people to overcome barriers and challenges related to emotions, coaches need to focus on intentional self-regulation. This is not therapy; it's investing in the social-emotional well being of adults in the same way that supporting children's social-emotional resiliency is important and a necessary life skill. The goal, first, is to support people to become aware of how their emotions and resulting actions are affecting their ability to achieve goals. Next, coaches want to help their coachees thoughtfully create plans for how they will change their emotional responses to be successful. Coaches can help people name and identify their emotions, recognize whether the emotions are getting in the way, and understand how emotions are contributing to or distracting them from getting where they want to go. The graphic on page 29 illustrates how beliefs and perceptions foster feelings and actions, which cause outcomes. Coaches help coachees link their ability to self-regulate and take responsibility for their thoughts, feelings, and actions. Then it is up to the coachee to implement action plans to be responsible for themselves, reframe responses, and modify their behaviors. Many coaches are uncomfortable talking about feelings with their coachees, but it is important to invest in the resilience of adults in the early childhood field, to strengthen their emotional self-regulation, because their emotional well-being is critical for them to model for, interact with, and respond positively to young children with a nurturing demeanor.

SUPPORTING ADULT LEARNERS WITH DARS

We can support adults in much the same way we do children—by promoting their social-emotional resilience. Coaches can help educators strengthen protective factors so they are better able to deal with stressors or emotional triggers. In addition, as they can gain more self-control and make better choices, they will improve their professional practices. In their book *Building Your Bounce: Simple Strategies for a Resilient You*, authors Mary Mackrain and Nefertiti Bruce Poyner offer a tool to help adults identify and assess their protective factors and areas of strength—the Devereux Adult Resilience Survey (DARS). This survey has twenty-three items, each one relating to thoughts and behavior that have been shown to support resilience. The information can be used to help individuals build on these strengths, such as creativity and setting limits, so they can better cope with adversity and the stresses of daily life. Statistical analysis shows that the DARS is an excellent tool for providing adults with an opportunity to gain valuable insights into the protective factors that contribute to their social-emotional well-being and personal strengths, as well as areas of need, particularly in these four areas:

Relationships: The mutual, long-lasting, back-and-forth bond we have with other people in our lives.

Internal beliefs: The feelings and thoughts we have about ourselves and our lives, and how effective we think we are at taking action in life.

Initiative: The ability to make positive choices and decisions and act upon them.

Self-control: The ability to experience a range of feelings and express them using the words and actions society considers appropriate.

I use the DARS to assess a coachee's strengths and to explore areas of needs in regard to their resilience, their ability to bounce back from adversity, and how this can strengthen their ability to achieve their desired results. You can download a DARS assessment from www.redleafpress.org /transformationalcoaching.

The purpose of the DARS is not to compare individuals' scores to the population but to give adults, more specifically teachers, the opportunity to become aware of personal strengths and areas of need. Upon completion of the Devereux Adult Resilience Survey, individuals are encouraged to use the *Building Your Bounce: Simple Strategies for a Resilient You* adult journal. This journal provides strategies for strengthening adults' protective factors that are shown to support resilience. It takes a fair amount of reflection and practice to change any negative thoughts you might have and to integrate new behaviors that are good for you.

An additional resource available from the Center for Resilient Children website is the Devereux Resilient Leadership Survey (DERLS), which was created to support leaders as they reflect on how to promote the capacity for resilience in early childhood educators. This survey is an excellent tool for coaches to use, both when they need to self-plan for supporting the resiliency of coachees and when they are coaching directors to implement strategies to intentionally promote and strengthen their staff's protective factors.

Devereux Adult Resilience Survey (DARS)

by Mary Mackrain

Take time to reflect on and complete each item on the survey below. There are no right answers! Once you have finished, reflect on your strengths and then start small and plan for one or two things that you feel are important to improve. For fun and practical ideas on how to strengthen your protective factors, use the chapters *Building Your Bounce: Simple Strategies for a Resilient You*

Items	Yes	Sometimes	Not Yet
Relationships			
1. I have good friends who support me.			
2. I have a mentor or someone who shows me the way.			
3. I provide support to others.			
4. I am empathetic to others.			
5. I trust my close friends.			
Internal Beliefs			
1. My role as a caregiver is important.			
2. I have personal strengths.			
3. I am creative.			
4. I have strong beliefs.			
5. I am hopeful about the future.			
6. I am lovable.			
Initiative			
1. I communicate effectively with those around me.			
2. I try many different ways to solve a problem.			
3. I have a hobby that I engage in.			
4. I seek out new knowledge.			
5. I am open to new ideas.			
6. I laugh often.			
7. I am able to say no.			
8. I can ask for help.			
Self-Control			
1. I express my emotions.			
2. I set limits for myself.			
3. I am flexible.			
4. I can calm myself down.			

Devereux Center for Resilient Children | 444 Devereux Drive, Villanova, PA 19085 | (866) 872-4687 | www.centerforresilientchildren.org

This can also be downloaded at https://centerforresilientchildren.org/wp-content/uploads/Devereux-Resilient-Leadership-Survey-DERLS.pdf (Wagner and Poyner 2016).

INCREASE EMOTIONAL SELF-REGULATION AND IDENTIFYING TRIGGERS

People who are not very emotionally self-regulated have problems with monitoring and regulating their emotional responses. For some this is a more generic way of being, while others struggle most around certain kinds of situations or specific triggering emotions. For example, some teachers are triggered by children spitting, cursing, being aggressive, or biting. In these situations, coaching can help teachers clarify what their specific trigger is, what underlying thoughts are causing such strong emotional responses, and how they can reframe this habitual dynamic. Share the following Trigger Teaching with coachees to educate and help them become aware of the inherent pattern at play when they are triggered by any situation. The accompanying What I Can Do When I Have Been Triggered activity is a tool to help them gain awareness and reflect on the thoughts underlying their emotional feelings, and then reframe those thoughts and choose alternative actions.

TRIGGER TEACHING

A trigger is anything another person says or does, or a material circumstance, that causes an emotional reaction in us, typically a very strong and/or disproportionate emotional reaction. When you are triggered your mind has a strong opinion—and sends a strong message—about what the trigger means about you. Then you have a strong feeling about what your mind is telling you. The trigger is only an issue—*not* the problem. The trigger is a button that got pushed and that points to a deeper belief or pain in you. Typically these are false beliefs we hold as true or old pains we carry around that are not yet healed. A trigger can be reframed not as a problem, but as a gift to foster deeper self-reflection. A trigger is always a clue that our state of consciousness has shifted toward an illusory or negative place. A trigger that happens over and over in different situations points to an area where our heart is closed.

☐ ☐

WHAT I CAN DO WHEN I HAVE BEEN TRIGGERED

Skill: How to change trigger thoughts to calming thoughts.

Activity: To remove your "buttons" that people or circumstances push.

1. Recognize that I have been triggered. Remember, the trigger is *never* the problem.

2. Be aware that my consciousness and mind-set have shifted in my reaction.

3. Ask myself, "What just happened that I reacted to?"

4. Identify what my mind is telling me about that situation or person.

5. Identify what feelings I have based on what my mind is telling me.

6. Acknowledge that while I'm upset, my inclination is to punish by _____, or to make the person feel bad by _____, or to blame _____.

7. Ask myself "what if" and "then what" questions about what my mind is saying.

    _____

    _____

8. If you can, shift your consciousness or mind-set back into the moment. Remind yourself you are not a victim to circumstances and other people's behaviors. Reframe your awareness and attitude toward wanting to be responsible for your thoughts, feelings, and responses.

    _____

    _____

9. If you can't shift your consciousness, take some actions to release the emotional and physical energy and calm yourself, such as using deep breathing, taking a walk, working out, dancing wildly to music, or meditating.

10. I want to feel better and be responsible. I accept and let go of my feelings (write in feeling words from step 5)

    _____

my thoughts that cause those feelings (write in trigger thoughts from step 4)

_____

and my need to be right and punish by (write in answers from step 6)

_____

11. What I really want to happen in this situation is . . . (use positive words only)

_____

_____

12. I am not really upset at this person or situation, but at my own thinking, my reaction, and, ultimately, myself for not knowing what to do or how to help.

13. I take responsibility, not blame, for all my actions, thoughts, and feelings in regard to (write person's name and/or situation)

_____

14. I forgive myself and now choose to connect with love instead of my upset.

One loving thought I can think about this person or circumstance is

_____

_____

One loving thought I can think about myself is

_____

_____

15. Thank you (person's name or circumstance)

_____

for teaching me (lessons learned)

_____

□ □

Busting Stress Obstacles and Barriers

Feeling stressed and overwhelmed is a common response to life's demanding pressures. Stress affects all aspects of our lives—physical, mental, emotional, and spiritual. What is stress? Hans Selye, the medical researcher who coined the term *stress*, defined it as the nonspecific response of the body to any demand for change. Any demand for change is pretty broad-reaching, so it's likely that most people who are receiving coaching are experiencing stress at some level, for they are trying to make changes and professional improvements. Here are several other definitions of stress:

- a mentally or emotionally disruptive or upsetting condition occurring in response to adverse external influences and capable of affecting physical health, usually characterized by increased heart rate, a rise in blood pressure, muscular tension, irritability, and depression

- a stimulus or circumstance causing such a condition

- a state of extreme difficulty, pressure, or strain

Following are four basic principles to transform stress and to become more capable of responding to the demands of stress in our lives:

1. Become response-able.
2. Start where you have choice.
3. Reframe perceptions to empower yourself.
4. Focus on what you want, not what you worry about—what you focus on expands.

TRANSFORM STRESS PRINCIPLE 1: BECOME RESPONSE-ABLE

The key to addressing stress is to recognize the pivotal relationship between all these demands and conditions listed in these definitions and our ability to respond to those demands. My approach to handling stress is to consider how stress is the result of demands and a person's level of ability to meet demands. You can think of this as a ratio.

$$STRESS \ is \ldots \quad \frac{Demands}{Ability \ to \ respond \ to \ demands}$$

A major factor influencing people's stress levels is how they perceive the level of control or choice they have. It's essential to identify where a coachee has a choice, as this empowers them to take necessary actions. Basically, a person has two choices for how to transform stress—either *decrease* the demands or *increase* their ability to respond to those demands. Therefore, it is critical to examine where you or your coachee do have choice and control in relationships, both to the demands and your ability to respond to demands.

To transform stress do the following:

1. DECREASE demands.
2. INCREASE ability to respond to demands.
3. REFRAME perceptions and responses.

We have 100 percent control over how we respond to demands. Our ability to respond is related to our ability to reframe perceptions, which is connected to our ability to regulate both our thoughts and our feelings; our physical state of well-being or health; our sense of being "connected," which can be viewed as both relational and spiritual; and our sense of efficacy—believing that what we do matters and that we can make a difference. All of these are modifiable.

Essentially, to expand one's capacity to choose more positive and proactive ways of responding to demands is within a person's control. I call this being "response-able." These are very similar to the protective factors that the DARS measures—internal beliefs, relationships, self-control, and initiative. By strengthening your protective factors, you increase your ability to respond to demands or risk factors. To become response-able is a major focus of transformational coaching. Coaches work to help people improve their response-ability by first moving from using intervention to prevention strategies, and then ultimately to using promotion strategies.

Intervention is the crisis-management approach used in chronic-stress situations. There will always be times when intervention may be necessary, but overall it's best to reduce the habitual cycles of being so stressed out. Typically coaches focus on helping coachees reduce negative or unsupportive thoughts and behaviors. When people get stuck at this level, often they are not aware of how their own thoughts and feelings are creating most of their stress—the stressor is their internal demands. They often mistakenly think the stressor is external and that they don't have choice and control; they are in reaction mode.

Prevention is the next step in becoming more response-able. This is when a person learns to anticipate upcoming stressors or challenges. A

Increase Response-Ability

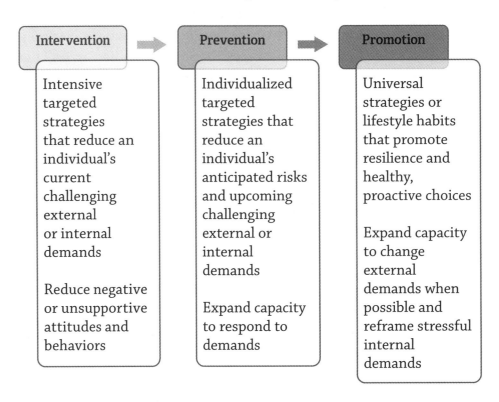

Intervention	Prevention	Promotion
Intensive targeted strategies that reduce an individual's current challenging external or internal demands	Individualized targeted strategies that reduce an individual's anticipated risks and upcoming challenging external or internal demands	Universal strategies or lifestyle habits that promote resilience and healthy, proactive choices
Reduce negative or unsupportive attitudes and behaviors	Expand capacity to respond to demands	Expand capacity to change external demands when possible and reframe stressful internal demands

coach's job is to help coachees create an action plan for dealing with demanding situations—whether from external or internal demands. In this step, coachees become more skillful at recognizing their problematic thought patterns that can be or are emotional triggers so they can prepare and prevent undesirable actions or reactions. This enables them to start responding instead of reacting.

Promotion is the master level of being response-able. These are people who have practiced strategies at the prevention level long enough that their actions have become positive habits they don't even have to think about. These positive practices have become such a routine way of living and working that these people are fairly poised when challenging and stressful situations occur. For example, they may incorporate daily mindfulness and reflective practices, exercise regularly, or eat well as a lifestyle routine. They have gained a lot of self-awareness. They have learned to reframe negative thinking and self-talk and are skillful at having positive, optimistic

"More resilient people tend to embrace love and friendship, count their blessings, and grow emotionally as a result of their hardships. . . . Learn to 'harness' the impact of stress on our emotions by . . . thinking in terms of challenges rather than threats, seeing ourselves as capable of meeting a challenge and thinking of the search for 'positive meaning' as a skill we can develop."
—Barbara Fredrickson, psychologist

thinking lead the way. All of these things increase their resilience and ability to bounce back easily when big demands and challenges come their way.

PREVENTION PRACTICE: BE PROACTIVE, *NOT* REACTIVE

1. Start with targeted **intervention** practices.

2. Identify and clarify upcoming external and internal demands, challenges, and anticipated risks, and build a plan as **prevention.**

3. Build lifestyle practices that **promote** resilience and expand your capacity for responding to demands.

PREVENTION PRACTICE: KNOW THYSELF . . .

What Are Your Stress Symptoms?

Increase your awareness of the symptoms that indicate when you are stressed so you can make preventive choices to shift from reacting at an intervention level and move toward a preventive, and eventually a promotional, level of response to stress.

List in the following areas symptoms that you experience when you are stressed.

Physical:

_____

_____

Mental:

_____

_____

Social-Emotional:

_____

_____

Spiritual:

_____

_____

□□□

TRANSFORM STRESS PRINCIPLE 2: START WHERE YOU HAVE CHOICE

It makes sense to focus time, energy, and effort on this lower part of the stress ratio—increase the ability to respond to demands—because this is where a person has the most choice and control, which can have profound results in shifting a person's experience of stress. But it is also worth discerning the difference between external and internal demands. People typically have little choice or control over external demands, perhaps less than 20 percent. Therefore, spending time complaining, focusing on, or trying to change external demands is not the wisest use of time, energy, or attention. Internal demands, on the other hand, are well worth focusing on since each person has 100 percent control over those! These are typically the values, beliefs, thoughts, and feelings that coaches help people become aware of and reframe when necessary. Managing and regulating internal demands is key to reducing stress levels.

Again, coachees can help people reduce and transform stress by reducing internal demands and increasing their ability to respond to demands. That is where a person has choice and control. These are the areas that coaches want to encourage coachees to explore and examine so they can make informed decisions and make viable action plans to bust stress barriers and obstacles. Use the worksheet on page 158 to help coachees reflect on their sources of stress and analyze whether the demands are external or internal.

TRANSFORM STRESS PRINCIPLE 3: REFRAME PERCEPTIONS TO EMPOWER YOURSELF

This principle was introduced in the Attitudes section earlier in this chapter. A key tool in reducing internal demands is to reframe limiting perceptions or negative attitudes. This affects the actions a person is both able and

DEMANDS	
External	Internal
<20% Control	100% Control
• Other people's expectations • Other people's actions • Job descriptions • Performance standards • Overload—too much to do in a specific time frame • Deadlines (that are nonnegotiable) • Weather • Traffic • Delayed flights • Bills	• Expectations of yourself • Values and beliefs • Negative or limiting attitudes • Disempowering perceptions • Overwhelm—emotional reaction to the overload of tasks or a to-do list • Self-judgment • Discouragement • Negative self-talk • Mental loops (worry)

willing to take, not only to make changes but to reduce and transform their experience of stress. Become aware of how your beliefs, thoughts, and feelings create your behaviors, actions, and habits. Increase your awareness of how the outcomes you are experiencing are linked to your choice in behaviors, which are motivated by your underlying beliefs, thoughts, and feelings.

▢▢▢

THE POWER OF PERSPECTIVE

Watch your **thoughts**. They create your feelings.

Watch your **feelings**. They become your actions.

Watch your **actions**. They become your habits.

Watch your **habits**. They become your character.

Watch your **character**. It becomes your destiny.

▢▢▢

TRANSFORM STRESS PRINCIPLE 4: FOCUS ON WHAT YOU WANT
I introduced this principle in the Attitudes section earlier in this chapter when discussing mental billboards. This is a tool that helps reframe

Common Sources of Stress and Demands

External

Major life events

Continuous and unpredictable change

Emergencies

Daily hassles

Emails

Poor relationships

Work or school

Other people's behaviors

Finances

Workload/overload—too much to do, too little time

Pressing deadlines

Demands from others

Traffic

Challenging or difficult relationships

Challenging behaviors of other people

Current events (war, poor economy, and so on)

Loss of job

New job or new responsibilities

What specific external demands are you currently facing that feel challenging to meet?

_____

_____

_____

_____

Internal

Emotions

Attitudes

Filters

Unexamined beliefs

Limiting perceptions

Expectations (of self and others)

Perfectionism

Judgments

Negative thoughts

Negative self-talk

Concepts or rules ("should" statements)

Overwhelm—emotional reaction to overload

Feeling pressure to be "on" 24/7

Fear of unemployment

Fear of forgetting something

Mental hamster wheel

Worry

What specific internal demands are currently contributing to your experience of concerns, overwhelm, or pressure?

_____

_____

_____

_____

attitudes and re-aim actions and habits to get the outcomes you want. It helps to identify that you do have choice and control over what you think, and over *what* you think about. You can use mental billboards to keep your attention on *what* to think and *where* to focus. Following are several prevention practices that are helpful both to increase awareness and increase a person's ability to proactively respond to life's demands and reduce stress.

☐ ☐

PREVENTION PRACTICE: STRESS REFLECTION ACTIVITY

Write a list of things that cause you stress or are current stressors in your life, both personally and professionally. Also list things that calm you down or that you can do to calm yourself. Be specific.

What currently stresses you?

_____

_____

_____

What calms you down?

_____

_____

_____

☐ ☐

Prevention Practice: Empty Out and REmember—Write It Down

Trying to remember all the details, to-dos, actions, and thoughts can cause a lot of disturbance, stress, and worry. Such lists keep people up at night, disturbing their sleep, which then compounds the level of stress. In addition, people create unrealistic to-do lists with so many items, they are impossible to accomplish in a day. This running to-do list also creates stress and is a common source of overwhelm—an emotional response to feeling like there is too much to do. Overload, on the other hand, is when we have a lot to get done in a certain time frame. This state is usually temporary and is related to an upcoming deadline or project. This is an important distinction to

Prevention Practice: Domains of Responsibility for Self-Management

All stress and external demands can't be stopped, but you can make choices about what you can control—yourself. Managing the internal demands we make of ourselves is a key practice for self-management and self-control. The following are strategies to manage stress.

Place a check mark next to the strategies that you have actually practiced in the *last* thirty days. Place an *X* next to the strategies you believe will be helpful for you in the *next* thirty days.

Personal

- ☐ Take a bath
- ☐ Take a walk
- ☐ Deep breathing
- ☐ Biofeedback
- ☐ Dance wildly

Physical

- ☐ Exercise
- ☐ Get enough sleep
- ☐ Eat and drink sensibly
- ☐ Drink water
- ☐ Stop smoking or other bad habits
- ☐ Muscle relaxation
- ☐ Take body breaks

Mental

- ☐ Use positive messages or create mental billboards
- ☐ Reframe limiting or negative thoughts and perspectives
- ☐ Examine your values and live by them
- ☐ Set realistic goals and expectations
- ☐ Use mental imagery for relaxation
- ☐ Don't work during meals
- ☐ Read a book
- ☐ Take a full twenty-four-hour break from any work once a week
- ☐ Take a "device abstinence day" regularly

Social-Emotional

- ☐ Do something you enjoy every day
- ☐ List what you are grateful for
- ☐ Release emotions appropriately
- ☐ Spend time with and talk to friends and family
- ☐ Calm your senses and emotions
- ☐ Build positive relationships with family, friends, and colleagues
- ☐ Ask for help
- ☐ Spend time with pets
- ☐ List your strengths and successes
- ☐ Listen to music
- ☐ Journal

Spiritual

- ☐ Identify your heart's deepest desire
- ☐ Take time to be involved in your spiritual community
- ☐ Meditate
- ☐ Study and practice relaxation or mindfulness techniques
- ☐ Take time to be in nature
- ☐ Pray
- ☐ Chant
- ☐ Take prayer walks
- ☐ Use mantras
- ☐ Spend quiet, peaceful time alone
- ☐ Attend a retreat

make—are you experiencing overload or overwhelm, or both? Some people can experience overload and be very calm about it, just doing their best to stay focused and get as much done as possible. They are experiencing overload but not overwhelm. Coaches can help people make this distinction and choose the appropriate strategies and tools to help, depending on the situation. If a person experiences chronic overload, it indicates that they likely need better time management skills and need to set more realistic goals and expectations; this would be a good avenue to pursue for helping them address this problem. If someone experiences chronic overwhelm, then exploring their emotional triggers and underlying thoughts is probably a good course of action. They may need more strategies to help them self-regulate and be calm.

One strategy for both overload and overwhelm is to make a distinction between a to-do list and a "REmember list" (RE list for short). A to-do list is related to the actual hours available to do tasks on a given day. For example, if you work from nine o'clock to five o'clock and are in meetings all morning until noon, then you have only five hours available for actions. You need to plan time to eat, travel if necessary, and do other required activities that also reduce actual work time. Your to-do list, then, needs to include only the items that can be accomplished in the actual hours you have available for that day. Most people collapse their to-do list and their RE list. A RE list is a list of all the things that need your attention or that you need to remember at some point. This is usually a longer list. I recommend writing your RE list in a notebook or paper that can be added to a three-ring binder. The to-do list items come from the RE list. For example, you wake up at three o'clock in the morning and remember you haven't picked up the dry cleaning. That would go on your RE list. In the morning, when you are making your to-do list, you have to look at your available time and decide whether that has to happen today or can wait until another day. If it needs to happen that day, then you need to be clear about what time you will do it that day and add it to your schedule—in time. Your RE list will always be changing, and you will cross things off as you transfer them to your to-do list and complete them. Separating these two lists (1) helps depressurize and calm your mind by transferring thoughts to a RE list and not jamming up your own thought process, (2) allows you to be more productive and feel more accomplished by having a realistic daily to-do list, (3) helps you recognize if you need additional strategies to manage your time and deal with overload, and (4) allows you to identify any strategies needed to deal with emotional overwhelm.

Take the next five minutes and practice emptying out your mind by writing any thoughts that come to your mind on the REmember list worksheet.

☐☐

THE RE-MEMBER LIST—EMPTY OUT AND WRITE IT DOWN

Write down anything on your mind. Here's a quick note before you begin: this is *not* a to-do list!

_____

_____

_____

_____

_____

_____

_____

☐☐

Busting Skill Obstacles and Barriers

PRACTICE AND REPEAT

Acquiring new skills or reinforcing known skills takes time and practice. Repetition, repetition, and repetition are key. It's not unlike the life of a toddler who is learning and practicing many newly acquired skills—they do it over and over again. They dump and fill buckets, they drop things off a high chair to test that the items always fall, they practice walking and fall down *a lot*! And we know from brain development that this repetition affects the patterning of the neural networks in the brain. Repetition or practice is how we create neural networks that build skill and strengthen habits.

While practice and repeatedly doing simple tasks or new behaviors is how we acquire and build skills, the process frequently involves plateaus where it doesn't seem like progress is happening. Tolerating these periods of level plateaus are key to having sustained change. Coaches can support the skill development process by first ensuring the coachee knows the information or skill set they need. So, both knowledge and skill are necessary. If either of these are lacking, then the first facilitation or scaffolding strategy will likely be teaching/tutoring or supporting the coachee in getting the professional development they need for a certain topic or content. Coaches can then use the Training Goal Plan Form to support coachees in identifying specific actions they want to implement based on the new knowledge or skill they learned.

Then supporting coachees to implement, experiment, and practice will be a big part of the coach's role. Helping them both to reflect on and create a plan for the repetition of the identified actions, which will become habits of skillful practice, would be part of the Mobilize stage of the GROOMER Framework for Change—to create an action plan to achieve the desired skill mastery. As coachees practice and possibly make mistakes in the Experiment stage of the GROOMER model, they will likely need encouragement, reframing any negative or limiting thinking that creeps in during this part of the skill-acquisition process.

MODIFY COACHING STRATEGIES BASED ON SKILL-TO-WILL RATIO

There is an important connection between people's willingness to change and their ability (skill) to actually do so. This is where motivation and skill intersect. It will be important for coaches to examine this skill-to-will ratio to discern which facilitation strategy will be most effective. Skill depends on a coachee's expertise, experience, training, understanding, and competency. Will depends on their desire to achieve, take initiative, and commit, and their feelings of safety and confidence. This is especially true when considering whether to choose a more or less directive facilitation tool and how to intentionally slide along the Continuum of Professional Development Facilitation Strategies. In his book *The Tao of Coaching*, Max Landsberg discusses the need to match your style of interaction with coachees' skills and their will and readiness for the task they are trying to accomplish. He offers a skill-to-will coaching interaction matrix that is helpful to make this choice. I've modified his matrix by adding the facilitation strategies from the continuum in parentheses (Landsberg 2015, 51).

	Low Skill	High Skill
High Will	GUIDE (Teach Consult)	DELEGATE (Mentor Coach)
Low Will	DIRECT (Teach Consult)	EXCITE (Mentor Coach)

The following is an overview of common skills early childhood educators need to acquire and develop mastery of to support CQI efforts personally and at the program level.

- Increase social-emotional skills of self-regulation, communication, relationship, and conflict resolution; these are often called *emotional intelligence skills*.

- Expand general skills related to a profession, job description, role, and responsibilities. This might differ for a program director; supervisor; coach; education specialist; home-site visitor; parent educator; infant/toddler, preschool, or school-age teacher or assistant; family child care provider; or parent.

- Support specific skill acquisition or mastery of field skills related to specific roles and responsibilities, such as grant writing, hiring/firing, adult education strategies, diaper changing, environment or classroom design, health practices, positive guidance and discipline, planning engaging activities, parent engagement, advocacy, routines, or adult-child interactions.

- Deepen mastery of specific early care or educational content, curriculum, disciplines, or assessments, such as a specific social-emotional curriculum, literacy, math, STEAM, infant/toddler programs, or Early Childhood Rating Scales.

FIVE GUIDELINES TO DEAL WITH HOMEOSTASIS

In his book *Mastery: The Keys to Success and Long-Term Fulfillment*, George Leonard writes, "The problem is, homeostasis works to keep things as they are even if they aren't very good" (1992, 110). He identifies homeostasis—a tendency to remain the same, which essentially translates into having a resistance to change—as a key problem that needs to be dealt with in order to achieve skill mastery. Mastering skills involves learning and practicing new habits repeatedly. It's really easy *not* to do this, to take no action or to start the process of learning a new skill or mastering an existing one and then gradually stopping the effort. This is the "don't rock the boat" mentality that needs to be addressed for change to happen. Leonard (1992, 114) offers five guidelines to help deal with homeostasis, to more easily make improvements, and, most importantly, to make those changes last:

1. Be aware of the way homeostasis works.
2. Be willing to negotiate with your resistance to change.
3. Develop a support system.
4. Follow a regular practice.
5. Dedicate yourself to lifelong learning.

A coach can be crucial in helping someone follow the five guidelines to deal with homeostasis, which touch on many points already discussed in this book:

1. Expand awareness of what's limiting success and, in this case, how easy it is to do nothing. It's usually easier than doing something.
2. Help people in whatever stage of readiness they are in to progressively overcome resistance to change and move into action and maintenance.
3. Become the coachee's support system through the coaching relationship. Helping people change and learn is the whole purpose of coaching.
4. Promote the implementation and practice of daily actions that, over time, help develop new skills and create habits. This is a major focus of how coaches support coachees through the Experiment and Refine components of the GROOMER Framework.
5. Commit to being a lifelong learner yourself, and both model and encourage educators to embrace CQI as a way of being a lifelong learner.

Change and skill mastery are all about taking one small step at a time, repeating them over and over—practicing actions over time until they become habits. This might be about implementing discipline practices that promote positive social-emotional protective factors or about how to facilitate reading circles with young children, change diapers, observe children and document progress, properly fill out an administrative form, or give performance reviews. Whatever the skill is, it will take practice and the attitude to tolerate the discomfort of learning a new way to do something.

Breaking or letting go of a habit is often needed to learn new and different practices. When I work with coaches to choose facilitation strategies that allow the coachee to reflect, gain awareness, and direct their own course for change, the coaches often report noticing how frequently they give advice or want to give a quick fix to a coachee. Changing this habit can be quite challenging. It requires a lot of awareness, practice, tolerance of mistakes, and modifying and refining actions. It will also require frequent reframing of negative or limiting thoughts and beliefs, especially those that are about how we think either our own or another's progress "should be" going, feelings of discouragement, or unsupportive internal or external expectations.

The more coaches practice changing their own professional practices, the better they will be able to facilitate this for others. Sharing with a coachee your own goals, struggles, progress, and how you managed and reframed your attitudes during the plateaus and the change process can be both trust building and very encouraging. Remember to respect whatever stage your coachee is currently at and use appropriate and intentional strategies and tools that match their willingness and risk tolerance to help them gain new skills and master existing skills so they can be more effective in their professional practices.

Take time to reflect on what you learned in this chapter and its impact on and value for you.

_____

_____

Key messages:

- **Awareness:** Reflection is the tool to expand awareness. Expand your ability to create the outcome you want by changing your responses to events using the E + R = O formula.
- **Attitudes:** Reframe disempowering perspectives. Use mental billboards to focus on what you want, not what you worry about.
- **Motivation:** Use the Costs and Payoffs activity to examine what's holding negative behaviors in place.
- **Emotions:** Increase self-regulation skills by using the DARS to assess and strengthen adult protective factors. Learn the trigger teachings and use them to reframe your responses.
- **Stress:** Become response-able and either increase your ability to respond to demands or decrease unnecessary internal demands. Be proactive, not reactive. Start where you have choice. Practice the following stress-management skills: complete the Stress Reflection activity, use the REmember list, and practice self-management to identify calming strategies in all four domains—mental, physical, emotional, and spiritual.
- **Skills:** Practice and repetition of simple tasks or new behaviors over time builds mastery of skills, aligns skill and will, and supports you as you overcome homeostasis and tolerate discomfort while learning.

Objective: What are key words or phrases, quotes, concepts, stories, activities, or ideas that stand out or stick for you personally?

_____

Reflective: What part of this feels affirming or inspiring? What aspect feels like a stretch or might be challenging for you?

_____

_____

Interpretive: What was most relevant and meaningful for you? How does this information affect your work or coaching practices?

_____

Decisional: What implications does this have for your actions in the future? What are you most committed to putting into action?

_____

Documentation: Making Transformation Visible

Documentation should focus on the process of change (how), the outcomes (what), and the status or progress of the transformation. Documenting progress includes collecting information about the goals, benchmarks, milestones, and modifications made along the way. Transformation is a journey, and the documentation record tells a story about that journey. It makes people's transformation visible to themselves and others. It reflects the desired destination, how they got there, what influenced them, and where they currently are. Documentation can serve as a form of research, an assessment tool, a valuable way to record learning and to inform decision-making. Documentation is not something that happens only at the end of a project, journey, or learning experience. It needs to be a window into the dynamic, transformational experience of growing, learning, and changing as it occurs during each stage of the process. Documentation plays a key role, for both the coach and coachee, to simply help remember what happened from a historical and procedural perspective. There are developmental stages of documenting the coaching experience. This chapter outlines a variety of forms that support data collection and documentation efforts. These forms offer different ways to document goals, action plans, and time frames; other forms address how to document the process of journeying through the GROOMER Framework of Change process. The forms can be accessed and downloaded online.

Documentation Methods

Documentation can take many forms. Some coaches start by assessing a coachee's strengths and taking written notes of coaching conversations, the coachee's goals, and action plans. Others explore additional methods for collecting data and information about the coaching experience, use progress reports, and discover ways to tell the story about the coachee's journey—all in an effort to support coachees in telling their own story. This process might include using the usual quantitative assessments results, such as scores from an Environmental Rating Scale (ERS), a CLASS assessment, or any other similar tools common in the early childhood field. To document coaching, I would encourage expanding the idea of documentation to include a variety of qualitative documentation tools that tell the transformation story about both early childhood educators (the coachee) and the coach. A more integrated approach could provide a holistic and humanistic view of the person's strengths and goals, what happened and why, and how this information can help both the coachee and coach think more deeply about their professional practices. In addition, the information collected and documented can be used as part of the learning and reflection process. Any kind of recorded documentation gives the coachee an avenue to gain perspective and learn from the information as a metacognitive tool. This information could include verbal, visual, or mixed media approaches to documentation.

- **Verbal:** This includes either written (notes, journals, broadcast boards, and so on) or spoken documentation, as in audio recordings, podcast journals, or feedback conversations.

- **Visual:** Using art, videos/photographs, and vision boards can add very important perspectives for expressing the learning process, reflecting about it, and assessing successes and accomplishments.

- **Mixed Media:** This might be something similar to the Learning Story approach that originated in New Zealand to tell the story of children's learning. This storytelling approach to learning can be used with early childhood educators and with the coaches themselves. Through a combination of media methods that serve as documentation, this approach offers a way to tell the story of how we know whether what we are doing is effective. This might include videos with a description of accomplishments or specific projects, and commentary on the importance of this and how it represents the coachee's progress or learning. Coaches, coachees, supervisors, colleagues, and even children or families could add their reflections and commentary to add dimension to the story.

This variety of storytelling methods can be collected for the coachee in a professional development portfolio, similar to a portfolio of children's work and learning. This can contribute to an educator's philosophy or story of themselves, deepen their frame of reference, and expand the lens through which they view themselves. This can help them see their capacity for change and their ability to direct their own learning.

Coaches should also create their own professional development portfolio. In addition to the documentation methods mentioned above, coaches could include the Colorado Coaching Competencies Self-Evaluation Checklist that they complete at the beginning and end of each year of coaching. This can be used to help craft their own professional development plan that they develop with their supervisors. Since coaching is a relatively new venture and professional role in field of early childhood education, it would add depth of knowledge and some reliability regarding the effectiveness of coaching if coaches, individually, and coaching initiatives, collectively, created documentation systems to support the professional development learning story of coaches, as well.

The Big Picture

Documentation is most powerful when multiple vantage points, perspectives, and voices are gathered and recorded. Both the coach and the coachee need to contribute information and share their perspectives of the coaching experience. It's important they each tell their story from their own learning experience, since both the coach and the coachee are learning through the coaching relationship. Both should also give feedback to each other and to other stakeholders about the successes or challenges of the coaching initiative. It's through documentation that all stakeholders can gather data and information to be evaluated and analyzed, as well as to inform reflection and to influence decision-making that affects the continuous quality improvement efforts of all individuals, teams, programs, and agencies involved.

Documentation Forms

This chapter includes several documentation forms that can be helpful for coaches and coachee. They are available both as a regular PDF to print for taking handwritten notes and as an editable PDF for typing directly into the form. Before completing any of these forms, I always first show the form to the coachee so they are aware of what I am doing and what information I am writing. I tell them that I will share a copy of the completed form with them after each coaching session. If I am meeting with them in person and handwriting the notes, I will either type the notes into the editable PDF version later and email the notes to the coachee or photocopy my handwritten notes and leave the coachee a copy. Sometimes handwriting is the most effective way to take notes in the moment to be fully present to the coachee. If I am meeting by phone or video conference and have the capacity to take notes on a computer or tablet during a meeting, then I use the editable PDF version of the form and type directly into the form. I can share the notes immediately by printing or emailing them to the coachee. This information is for them, and sharing it with them increases the likelihood that they will become more engaged in and responsible for their own learning. It also helps them be more accountable since they have a written record of what actions they are going to take and by when. It is particularly important that any actions the coachee will be taking are given to them immediately. For example, provide them with a copy of the Action and Status Report at the completion of each session, and if that isn't possible, then certainly within twenty-four hours. Coaches are often required to enter notes into their program database, and these forms can be useful for reporting pertinent information; often they can be uploaded.

In addition to the forms described below, the online appendix at www .redleafpress.org/transformationalcoaching includes the Facilitation Activities and Forms included throughout this book. All forms available online are listed on page 181–83. The documentation forms outlined in this chapter are grouped into four categories:

1. **Goals and Mobilize Planning:** These are all optional forms. They each have a unique purpose, and you might find that one form works better for one coachee or program than another. Experiment and see which ones work the best for you.

   o The Goal and Targeted Action Plan Form is a basic form that helps clarify goals, measurable criteria for success, and goal actions to achieve the goal. It also includes places to consider potential challenges in achieving the goal, possible solutions to those challenges, and the Targeted Action Plan to overcome the identified challenges.

   o The Long- and Short-Term Goal Plan Form is to plan both long-term (six months or more) and short-term (one to five months) goals, as well as indicate the criteria for success.

   o The SMART Goal Worksheet creates a structure for developing goals that are specific, measurable, achievable, relevant, and timely.

   o The Storyboard Planning Approach Worksheet is a planning strategy used for detailing the sequential steps needed to achieve a specific goal and outcome.

o　The Training Goal Action Plan Form is designed to be completed after a coachee attends any training or professional development opportunity. It helps clarify the goals and actions coachees want to implement that they learned on any formal or informal educational occasion. This can then be used by the coach to support coachees to implement their plans.

2. **Documenting Progress and Accountability:** The first two forms are what I use in every coaching session to document progress and track accountability. The third form is optional.

o　The Action Plan and Status Report is a basic form that allows coaches to document and track different actions a coachee is going to take with a time frame for doing so. The form includes space to document the coachee's status and progress toward completing each action. Typically new information is added to this form during subsequent coaching sessions, tracking the status of current actions and the addition of any new ones. This form has three variations:

◊　The Action Plan and Status Report: Individual (used with an individual coachee)

◊　The Action Plan and Status Report: Team (used with a team of coaches)

◊　The Action Plan and Status Report: With Goal (used to identify a specific goal and corresponding actions to achieve it)

o　The GROOMER Framework for Change Progress Documentation Form provides space to document information about the coachee's progress in each of the seven components of the GROOMER framework. It is available in both a simple version for taking quick notes and a more detailed version to document more-specific information. See pages 58–60 for a completed sample of this form.

o　The GROOMER Framework for Change: Notetaking shows the model with write-on lines that coaches can use to take brief handwritten notes during a session. Coaches can write corresponding notes right on the components of the form as the coachee is sharing. This form is helpful to make summary notes, which can then be expanded with more details at a later date.

3. **Assessing Coachee Outcomes and Progress**

○   The Coachee Self-Reflection and GROOMER Progress Documentation Form is to be completed by coachees. Give it to them at the beginning of a coaching relationship to complete in stages along the way. For coachees who have more experience being coached, this form serves as a self-coaching tool, prompting them to consider the basic GROOMER Framework components throughout their current coaching project or area of focus. It includes a summary of the GROOMER components and instructions for how to complete the form.

4. **Assessing Coach Outcomes and Progress**

○   The Coach's Self-Reflection Form provides an opportunity for coaches to reflect on their own professional practices. It can be used to prepare for a coach's performance review or to create goals and action plans.

○   The Coach's Self-Reflection—Do More/Do Less Worksheet is a quick tool that helps coaches develop a reflective habit to consider what happened in a coaching session and what they might want to do more or less of. It helps coaches develop the skill of assessing their effectiveness and ways to make improvements.

○   The Coachee Evaluation of Coaching Session Form is designed to be completed by the coachee to provide the coach with feedback. It's best if the coachee can complete and return this to a coaching supervisor rather than to the coach directly. The supervisor can then combine all the feedback for the coach so it is anonymous. Another way to gather this information anonymously is to use these questions to create an online survey (using a service like SurveyMonkey, for example) that coachees can complete. It's best to have coachees complete this form once or twice a year. It empowers coachees to voice their feedback and informs coaches of ways they might improve. When a coach gives this evaluation to all their coachees, the results may reveal patterns of comments that indicate habits or styles in need of change.

○   The Coachee Feedback Form for Coaching Initiative is similar to the Coachee Evaluation of Coaching Session Form but is designed for use by a program to collect data to assess the effectiveness of individual coaches as well as the coaching initiative. It is a template that can be modified to meet individual program needs. Some programs collect this information to share with funders, to tell a more personal story of the coaching experiences. This is why there is a question asking if coachees give their consent to share their information using their name or not.

o Coaching Competencies for Colorado Early Childhood Education: A Self-Evaluation Checklist is based on the Colorado Coaching Competencies. Coaches can use it to evaluate their skills and competencies. It can also be used by a supervisor observing a coach in the field. This checklist and a copy of the Colorado Coaching Competencies are available free to download at www.cocoaches.net.

These forms enable coaches to self-assess their own practices and to gather information from others about their effectiveness—a crucial objective of this book. The intention is to help you deepen your reflective habits, collect and use data and documentation to inform your own professional journey, and take initiative to expand your coaching skills. It's important that coaches ask themselves, "How do I know if what I'm doing is working?" This is the foundational question—to continue to inform the desire and commitment to continually get better at getting better. This is how coaches walk their talk and demonstrate their commitment to improving their professional practices. Hopefully the GROOMER Framework for Change has provided you with a model not only to facilitate the transformation and learning of your coachees, but also to use as a map for traveling along your own professional development journey of change.

Reflection in Action

Reflect on what you learned in this chapter and its impact on and value for you.

_____

_____

_____

_____

_____

Key messages:

- Document the process, outcomes, and progress of the coaching experience to make transformation visible.
- Documentation is a form of research, an assessment tool, and a metacognitive tool.
- Use a variety of documentation methods, including verbal, visual, and mixed media to tell the story of both the coachee's and coach's journeys.
- A variety of documentation tools are described and provided in four categories: goals and mobilize planning, documenting progress and accountability, assessing coachee outcomes and progress, and assessing coach outcomes and progress.

Objective: What are key words or phrases, quotes, concepts, stories, activities, or ideas that stand out or stick for you personally?

_____

_____

Reflective: What part of this feels affirming or inspiring? What aspect feels like a stretch or might be challenging for you?

_____

_____

Interpretive: What was most relevant and meaningful for you? How does this information affect your work or coaching practices?

_____

_____

Decisional: What implications does this have for your actions in the future? What are you most committed to putting into action?

_____

_____

Conclusion

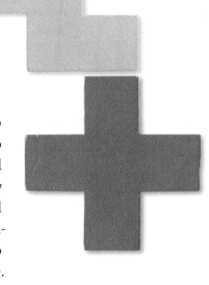

Relationships are the foundation for all learning. The coaching relationship is a unique opportunity to foster lifelong learning and inspire educators to reignite their passion for working in the field and hone their professional skills. A coach's role is to empower people to learn *how* to reflect and *how* to thoughtfully make data-driven decisions to improve their professional practices, solve their own problems, and be responsible for their own learning by learning *how* to change. As Alvin Toffler comments, the ability to unlearn and keep learning is foundational to being successful in this age. To learn is to change, and by changing we learn. The purpose of transformational coaching is to facilitate meaningful change. Exploring the role of a coach as a change agent is a strong theme throughout this book. Facilitating change requires focused, intentional decision-making about when to use which facilitation strategies and tools to meet the individual needs of the learner or coachee. Learning to differentiate between consulting and coaching strategies is key to purposefully sliding along the continuum in coaching conversations. Being able to discern when to use the more directive strategies associated with teaching and consulting and when to choose the less directive strategies associated with mentoring and coaching adds dimension and mastery to the art of coaching. Mastery is the result of practice, repetition, tolerance for the discomfort of learning from trial and error, and developing habits by taking small steps that, repeated daily over time, ultimately lead to sustainable change.

Reflection is the heart of transformational coaching and the foundation of the GROOMER Framework for Change model. Transformational coaching expands a coach beyond just being a content knowledge expert to being a change agent who facilitates reflection and transfers power to the coachee as often as possible. This, in turn, helps coachees self-modify their professional practices, reframe their underlying beliefs and thoughts, and ultimately achieve their desired results. The GROOMER model provides coaches with

"The illiterate of the 21st century will not be those who cannot read and write, but those who cannot learn, unlearn, and relearn."
—Alvin Toffler

a mental model to guide the reflective journey of change and to navigate the inquiry process of knowing what to ask questions about by investigating each of the seven components. This systematic, practice-based approach helps coaches be proactive thinkers and accountability partners with their coachees.

Coaching is a complex and adaptive endeavor that requires creativity and the ability to problem solve. Indeed, being a successful coach demands more than just implementing policies and procedures. Learning and implementing an array of facilitation strategies and coaching tools is essential to being proficient at cocreating relationships, communicating effectively, increasing awareness, fostering critical thinking, facilitating learning and results, and managing and documenting progress. A variety of practical universal and targeted strategies and tools have been offered throughout this book to expand a coach's resources to meet the diverse needs of coachees. When coaches are adept in these competency domains, they can empower coachees to become more response-able for their actions and increasingly capable of responding to the demands and challenges they face. To be effective, coaches have to do their own work to become self-aware, improve the quality of their professional practices, and essentially walk their talk. It's critical to build strong reflective habits to examine one's own life and professional practices, and to recognize and evaluate whether one's choices of approach, strategies, and tools are indeed facilitating learning and change in others. Coaches can use the GROOMER model to guide their own reflective process and to collect and examine data to make decisions to deepen their own professional development. This can be achieved not only by reflecting but also by gathering feedback from coachees about the effectiveness of the coaching relationship. Being responsible for one's own professional development is important not only for one's own growth and for the success of the coachee, but also to contribute to the advancement of coaching in the field of early childhood education.

Whether you are new to coaching or have years of experience, I hope you have found this model helpful and have learned and will practice these strategies and tools as you pursue your journey of continuous exploration, investigation, and quality improvement. Expand your knowledge, skills, and experience, and deepen your professional practices about how to facilitate change in yourself and others by taking the time to reflect, practice, and refine solutions—that's what real, sustainable change requires. Children deserve to have committed, thoughtful, respectful, and skillful educators who nurture, challenge, and inspire them. Each child needs someone who can see and polish the gem within them. Likewise, each educator deserves to have a support system and committed coaches who can do and model the same for them. Use this transformational coaching approach to do that and to help coachees get better at getting better. The world needs conscious people to contribute their gifts and model care for others. Thank you for investing your time to read this book, to be reflective, and to plan and cultivate your coaching skills. Hopefully you will bloom boldly.

Index of Reproducible Forms

Forms available at www.redleafpress.org/transformationalcoaching

Motivation

Identifying Cost–Payoff Activity Worksheet

Emotions

Devereux Adult Resiliency Survey (DARS)

Devereux Resilient Leadership Survey (DERLS)

Trigger Teaching and Activity Worksheet

Stress

Know Thyself . . . What Are Your Stress Symptoms Worksheet

Common Sources of Stress and Demands Worksheet

Stress Reflection Activity—What Stresses and Calms You Worksheet

The REmember List—Empty Out and Write It Down Worksheet

Domains of Responsibility for Self-Management Worksheet

Chapter 7—Reflection in Action

Chapter 8—Documentation: Making Transformation Visible

Goals and Mobilize Planning

Goal and Targeted Action Plan Form

Long- and Short-Term Goals

SMART Goal Worksheet

Storyboarding Planning Approach Worksheet

Training Goal Action Plan

Documenting Progress and Accountability

Action and Status Report—Individual

Action and Status Report—Team

Action and Status Report with Goal

GROOMER Framework for Change Progress Documentation—Brief Form

GROOMER Framework for Change Progress Documentation—Detailed Form

GROOMER Framework for Change Visual Graphic for Notes

Assessing Coachee Outcomes and Progress

Coachee Self-Assessment and GROOMER Progress Documentation

Assessing Coach Outcomes and Progress

Coach's Self Reflection—Do More /Do Less Worksheet

Coach's Self Reflection Form

Coachee Evaluation of Coaching Session

Coachee Feedback Form for Coaching Initiative

Chapter 8—Reflection in Action Form

References

Canfield, Jack. 2015. *The Success Principles: How to Get from Where You Are to Where You Want to Be*. 10th ann. ed. New York: HarperCollins.

Center on the Develping Child at Harvard University. 2017. "Deep Dives: The Science of Adult Capabilities." Accessed February 15, 2018. https://developingchild.harvard.edu/science/deep-dives/adult-capabilities.

Colorado Coaching Consortium. 2009. "Coaching Competencies for Colorado Early Childhood Education." March. www.cocoaches.net/uploads/Coaching_competencies_Oct_2010.pdf.

———. 2018. "Coaching Competencies for Colorado Early Childhood Education: A Self-Evaluation Checklist." December 16. www.cocoaches.net/uploads/colorado_competencies_for_early_childhood_coaches.pdf.

Daly, Lisa, and Miriam Beloglovsky. 2015. *Loose Parts: Inspiring Play in Young Children*. St. Paul, MN: Redleaf Press.

Drummond, Tom. 2002. *Connecting to Children: Guide to the Modules*. Seattle: Perf-ECT Performances for Early Childhood Teachers.

Elmore, Paul. 2011. "9 Most Common Automatic Negative Thoughts That Make Life Harder." www.paulelmore.com/therapeuticprocess/ants.

Heidemann, Sandra, Beth Menninga, and Claire Chang. 2016. *The Thinking Teacher: A Framework for Intentional Teaching in the Early Childhood Classroom*. Golden Valley, MN: Free Spirit Publishing.

Hine, Constant. 2011. *Creating Ease in a Day's Work Sign Book*. Lakewood, CO: Horizons In Learning. www.constanthine.com.

———. 2014. *Engaging Adult Learners Using Multiple Intelligences: The Toolkit of Adult Education Instructional Strategies*. Redmond, WA: Exchange Press.

Joyce, Bruce, and Beverly Showers. 2002. *Student Achievement through Staff Development*. 3rd ed. Alexandria, VA: Association for Supervision & Curriculum Development.

Landsberg, Max. 2015. *The Tao of Coaching: Boost Your Effectiveness at Work by Inspiring and Developing Those around You*. London: Profile Books.

Lavery, Cathryn, and Allen Brouwer. 2017. *SELF Journal*. BestSelf Co., LLC. https://bestself.co/pages/self-journal-pdf.

Leonard, George. 1992. *Mastery: The Keys to Success and Long-Term Fulfillment*. New York: Plume.

Levine, Hallie. 2015. "Be Your Own Life Coach: 7 Techniques to Live Your Dreams." *Yoga Journal*. January 7. www.yogajournal.com/lifestyle /life-coach-7-steps-realizing-dreams.

Mackrain, Mary, and Nefertiti Bruce Poyner. 2013. *Building Your Bounce: Simple Strategies for a Resilient You*. 2nd ed. Lewisville, NC: Kaplan Early Learning Company.

McKay, Matthew, Martha Davis, and Patrick Fanning. 2007. *Thoughts and Feelings: Taking Control of Your Moods and Your Life*. 3rd ed. Oakland, CA: New Harbinger Publications.

Mezirow, Jack. 1996. "Contemporary Paradigms of Learning." *Adult Education Quarterly* 46 (3). https://doi.org/10.1177/074171369604600303.

National Association for the Education of Young Children (NAEYC) and National Association of Child Care Resource & Referral Agencies (NACCRRA). 2011. *Early Childhood Education Professional Development: Training and Technical Assistance Glossary*. www.naeyc .org/sites/default/files/globally-shared/downloads/PDFs/our-work /public-policy-advocacy/glossarytraining_ta.pdf.

National Center on Quality Teaching and Learning. 2011. *School Readiness for All Children: Using Data to Support Child Outcomes*. National Center on Quality Teaching and Learning. Washington, DC: U.S. Department of Health and Human Services, Administration for Children and Families, Office of Head Start.

Nelson, Wayne, and Jo Nelson. 2017. *Getting to the Bottom of ToP: Foundations of the Methodologies of the Technology of Participation*. Bloomington, IN: iUniverse.

Olson, Jeff. 2013. *The Slight Edge: Turning Simple Disciplines into Massive Success & Happiness*. 8th ann. ed. Plano, TX: Success Books.

Prochaska, James O., John C. Norcross, and Carlo C. DiClemente. 1994. *Changing for Good: A Revolutionary Six-Stage Program for Overcoming Bad Habits and Moving Your Life Positively Forward*. New York: HarperCollins.

Stober, D. R. and Grant, A. M. eds. 2006. "Toward a Contextual Approach to Coaching Models." *Evidence Based Coaching Handbook: Putting Best Practices to Work for Your Clients*. 355–65. Hoboken, NJ: John Wiley & Sons.

Terrell, James Bradford, and Marcia Hughes. 2008. *A Coach's Guide to Emotional Intelligence: Strategies for Developing Successful Leaders*. San Francisco: Pfeiffer.

Wagner, Rachel, and Nefertiti Bruce Poyner. 2016. *The Devereux Resilient Leadership Survey (DERLS)*. Villanova, PA: The Devereux Foundation.

Young, Billie. 2017. *Continuous Quality Improvement in Early Childhood and School Age Programs: An Update from the Field*. BUILD Initiative. June. https://qrisnetwork.org/sites/all/files/conference-session /resources/Continuous%20Quality%20Improvement%20in%20 Early%20Childhood%20and%20School%20Age%20Programs.pdf.